PAUSE POINTS

ILLINI CHRISTIAN MINISTRIES, Inc.

PAUSE POINTS

THE MINDFUL PURSUIT OF HEALTH AND WELL-BEING

Gene Harker MD PhD
with
Curt Smith

WESTBOW
P R E S S
A DIVISION OF THOMAS NELSON

WestBow Press books may be ordered through booksellers or by contacting:

WestBow Press
A Division of Thomas Nelson
1663 Liberty Drive
Bloomington, IN 47403
www.westbowpress.com
1-(866) 928-1240

Because of the dynamic nature of the Internet, any Web addresses or links contained in
this book may have changed since publication and may no longer be valid. The views
expressed in this work are solely those of the author and do not necessarily reflect the
views of the publisher, and the publisher hereby disclaims any responsibility for them.

Any people depicted in stock imagery provided by Thinkstock are models,
and such images are being used for illustrative purposes only.

Certain stock imagery © Thinkstock.

Cover Design by Jeff Miller

ISBN: 978-1-4497-1015-6 (sc)
ISBN: 978-1-4497-1016-3 (hc)
ISBN: 978-1-4497-1017-0 (e)

Library of Congress Control Number: 2010942186

Printed in the United States of America

WestBow Press rev. date: 2/8/2011

In this book, I have tried to be positive but evenhanded in what I have written. While there are clear connections between how individuals live their lives and their health and well-being, there are no 100 percent guarantees. An optimist may experience better health (see chapter 2) and those with positive relationships may live longer (see chapter 1), but this is not always the case. My goal is to highlight ways to experience better health and well-being, but I cannot predict what will happen in the life of a particular individual. Health is complicated and involves many factors not covered in this book.

Also, in the pages that follow, I am not offering specific treatment advice for any particular medical or psychological illness. If you have a physical or mental problem, seek the care of a qualified healthcare professional.

To God,
who is the Author of all that is good

To Mom and Dad
who teach, by the way they live life,
what it means to be well

To Lynette, Alex, and Hayleigh
who are, for me, the *sine qua non* of health and well-being

Contents

Preface

Perhaps you have noticed how easy it is to get distracted and allow our health to slip. It is not that we consciously decide to risk our well-being. We do not plan to gain weight, alienate our friends, or sabotage our happiness. But in spite of good intentions and herculean effort, we cannot always find the health, happiness, and satisfaction we desire.

When it comes to transcending the mundane and getting the most out of each day, it is easy to lose focus and stray from the desired path. We begin relationships with idealistic optimism and a beautifully imagined future but soon find ourselves angry, alienated, and stressed. We set out in our profession ready to make a difference, but it quickly becomes a struggle to get up in the morning. We begin our journey with every intention of flourishing and passionately seeking the best, yet we find ourselves in survival mode—merely getting by.

Fortunately, it does not have to be this way. It is possible to seamlessly integrate healthy, life-giving practices into our daily lives. Growing scientific support links many of our everyday activities to tangible positive health outcomes.

Based on more than twenty-five years of professional experience as a psychologist, physician, and professor, and tempered by my personal experiences as a friend, father, and husband, I have come to believe health is found at the intersection of *mindfulness* and *purpose*. Those who live well immerse themselves in the present, fully engaged in the moment, while simultaneously considering where they would like to be in the future.

Health is discovered when we savor each moment and purposely do what we were made to do. And because we are biological, psychological, social, and spiritual beings, we are at our best when our efforts to live well involve every aspect of who we are. Health is certainly found in more obvious places like what we eat and how much we exercise, but it is also found in some rather surprising places like our friendships, our thoughts, our efforts to help others, and even our spirituality.

The active businesswoman finds health when she leaves the day's stress at the door and focuses intently on her three-year-old daughter, knowing both of them are better because of these precious connecting moments. The middle-aged man experiences health when he pauses to eat a nutritious lunch during his busy day, carefully selecting the right foods and mindfully experiencing every flavor, texture, and aroma. Health is also observed in the lives of individuals who are optimistic, appreciate their blessings, and believe they are valuable.

In this book, I identify seven essentials of health and well-being. These essentials point us toward a holistic, health-filled existence. They represent a broad cross-section of life, touching on many dimensions of our experience, including our interactions with others, our minds, our diets, our exercise activities, our approach to managing stress, and our faith. When we embrace these essentials as our own and begin to nurture them, we find ourselves in the midst of a life-enhancing journey that leads naturally to a sense of peace and well-being.

However, knowing the destination does not ensure our success. A beautifully imagined endpoint is only the beginning of our journey; we also need a map, or more accurately, a process to guide us. As I researched and wrote this book, I developed an approach to reaching our health-related goals called *Pause Points*. A Pause Point is a moment in time when we intentionally slow our pace, reflect on where we are, dream about where we would like to go, and experience a whole new direction.

Some Pause Point moments are quite dramatic like the middle-aged man whose drinking has wrecked his family, ruined his career, and forced him to live on the street. He wakes one morning reeking of alcohol and his own urine and can no longer deny he has a problem that is decimating his life. He vows to stop drinking and begins to use the resources available to make a change.

Most Pause Points, however, are less remarkable, fitting seamlessly into our everyday life. They are as simple as taking a walk, helping a co-worker, or connecting with a friend.

While very diverse, all Pause Points have one thing in common: they all influence our health. Every time we slow our pace and alter our course, our lives are affected and our well-being is enhanced or diminished, depending on the path we choose. The challenge is to know the path that will take us in the right direction.

In the pages that follow, you are introduced to a number of Pause Point experiences designed to help you get the most out of each day. As you proceed, slow your pace and take the time to mindfully engage in the exercises offered. Each exercise is designed as an experiment in which you are the sole participant. Try the suggestions and then observe their impact on your behaviors, thoughts, and feelings.

It is my hope *Pause Points* will initiate a life-long inspirational journey of self-discovery and personal well-being.

Acknowledgments

Writing *Pause Points* was a team effort. There are many who deserve special recognition, beginning with my wife and children. They freely allowed me to spend countless hours on this project and truly are my inspiration. Curt Smith, who wrote this book with me, was instrumental in helping me clarify and organize many of the concepts you will encounter in the pages that follow. Special thanks is due Sue Bondurant, Jason Anhalt, Mike Frasure, Dr. Graham Carlos, and Dr. Debbie Abel for their many insightful comments on earlier drafts. I would also like to thank Dr. J.K. Jones, Doug Felton, John Sima, Kevin Hazelwood, Dr. Mark Moore, and Jon Huskins who made the effort to ask about this project, providing much-needed encouragement. I am indebted to Ashley Woehler from IBJ Book Publishing and Jennifer Taylor for their expert editorial help. Their insights and ideas improved the manuscript at various stages of its development. I also appreciate the many contributions made by the staff of Westbow Press. They helped polish, refine, and shape this book into its final form.

GETTING STARTED

Introduction

Getting Started

Two roads diverged in the wood, and I—
I took the one less traveled by,
And that has made all the difference.
—Robert Frost

This was not at all how he imagined it.

After spending a sleepless night taking an inventory of his life, Jerry came to the sobering conclusion: he was heading in the wrong direction. In relationships, where he once experienced intimacy, he now felt strain and alienation. Work no longer captured his imagination like it once did. Instead of exercising in the early morning, he now slept in. And his faith, which had been a critical integrating force in his life, had moved to the periphery, a barely recognizable add-on to Jerry's harried existence. With his blood sugar creeping up, his pants growing snug, and his cholesterol rising, Jerry feared he would return from his next doctor's visit with a fistful of prescriptions.

Jerry's story is all too often our story. The ideal self we dream about is miles from the real self we experience on a day-to-day basis. If we pause to reflect on our health and well-being, it is not unusual to discover we have strayed from the desired path.

It is not that we intentionally set out to ruin our relationships, gain too much weight, or become cynical. We did not sit down one day and say, "I'm going to get off track and start doing things that will lead to a miserable existence." Rather, the change begins as a subtle, insidious shift. The demands of a fast-paced life begin to squeeze out our good intentions. We want to live well, but work is making too many demands. We hope to make it to the gym, but our time is consumed by laundry, dishes, and paying the bills. Survival becomes the goal and any hope for flourishing is reserved for the elite few—you know, the ones living on the other side of the fence where the grass is greener.

Fortunately, this does not have to be the case. It is possible to reverse this trend and begin a different experiential journey. This book is about resisting external factors that might impose an unhealthy direction, finding meaning and purpose, and then living in harmony with that purpose. It is written for those who desire to enjoy life and savor each moment along the way.

Based on a growing body of literature, and informed by my professional and personal experiences, I have come to believe well-being is found by individuals who live *mindfully* and *purposefully*. It is the companion of those who immerse themselves in whatever is in front of them at any given moment without losing their identity or direction in life. This kind of health is demonstrated by the busy doctor who sets aside her packed schedule to hold the hand of a patient facing a life-threatening illness, choosing in that moment to share meaningful human touch. It is observed in the practitioner of faith who frequently pauses to pray and meditate, seeking an intimate connection with God. Health is a whole-person experience, intentionally lived in the here and now.

A few years ago, I was invited to join some dear friends for a five-day hiking trip in the Grand Canyon. As I hiked down the trail that first morning, with a cool, gentle breeze blowing against my face, I was transfixed by the unparallel beauty that surrounded me. The cerulean, cloudless sky formed the perfect border for the rock formations with their many-colored hues. It was a rich sensory experience filled with incredible moments of awe and wonder.

Healthy living is like hiking the Canyon; those who live well know where they are going, but they are in no hurry because the journey itself has its own intrinsic rewards. While it is purposeful, with clear destinations and benchmarks, the fun is found along the way. Those who desire to get the most out of each day have a destination, a desired future in mind, but they live fully engaged in the present moment.

Strangely, however, living well is not automatic or linear. Common sense tells us that it should be simple—but it is not. The default path in life often leads to isolation, alienation, strife, angst, and ill health. We all know how easy it is to experience disharmony. Who has not screamed at another person, felt the pain of isolation, or eaten too much junk food?

One of the most widely accepted generalities of modern psychology is "bad is stronger than good."[1] There is consistent and compelling evidence suggesting that negative events have a more pronounced and lasting impact than positive events. The soldier exposed to a horrific battle lasting only a few minutes can be affected for the remainder of his life. Similarly, the child who was the victim of abuse can face significant issues well into adulthood. There is little, if any, doubt that traumatic experiences are life altering. But contrast this with positive experiences. While trauma has a lasting impact, there is no comparable counterpart when it comes to positive experiences. No matter how much pleasure is gained from a particular event, its positive impact is fleeting.

Even when we look at more mundane day-to-day occurrences, the impact of negative events lasts longer and is felt more intensely than the impact of their positive counterparts. A thoughtless, angry word from a friend can literally end that friendship, while the impact of a positive word lasts only for a brief moment before we are off to the next thought or feeling. A botched presentation at work may become the focus of our obsession for days, while the glow of a successful project is often barely noticeable. The beautiful, awe-inspiring sunrise we see during our morning commute is gone the instant we are cut off in traffic. It seems we are wired to feel more intensely and think more critically about our negative experiences.

So, how can we experience the health and well-being we desire? If we are not automatically predisposed to healthy living, and if bad is stronger than good, is it hopelessly romantic to dream of anything more than merely getting by?

Seven Essentials of Health and Well-Being

I believe it is possible to live well and get the most out of each day. I am discovering that well-being is found by those who mindfully and purposefully pursue seven essentials of health and well-being.

Seven Essentials of Health and Well-Being

- Love the Ones You're With
- Fill Your Mind with the Best
- Bring Out the Best in Others
- Eat Mindfully
- Exercise Faithfully
- Find Peace and Relaxation
- Connect with the Creator

These essentials represent a broad cross-section of our lives, including our relationships, our minds, our efforts to help others, our nutrition, our level of fitness, our ability to manage stress, and our spirituality. When we allow these essentials to determine our course, we begin to experience the peace and happiness we long for.

In the next few pages, I provide a brief overview of each essential. As you read through this section, make it as individual and personal as possible; consider the impact of these essentials on your life. Begin to look for how mind, body, and soul are uniquely interconnected in you.

Love the Ones You're With

Jerry Lewis (from the Timberlawn Research Foundation), a leading expert in social interactions, writes, "It is easy to forget that life is lived in relationships, and the quality of those relationships has much to do with how life turns out."[2] Personal experience teaches us this statement is indeed true. Who has not felt as if their heart was being ripped out when jilted by a loved one? Or, on the other hand, who has not been uplifted by a kind word from a mentor, respected colleague, or friend? When it comes to living well, relationships matter.

Chapter one of this book focuses on the process of creating a positive, supportive social network. In this chapter, I propose that *encouragement, engagement, caring, communication, excitement, good fences,* and *synergy* are consistently found in healthy relationships. After introducing these important relational qualities, I will lead you through a series of exercises to evaluate your social interactions and make changes where appropriate.

Fill Your Mind with the Best

In much of the Western world, there is a predisposition to view mind and body as separate, unrelated entities. In this view, mental processes and physical processes occur simultaneously, but they do not significantly interact. Recently, however, this belief has been challenged. There is growing evidence of a meaningful connection between what is going on in our minds and our physical health and well-being.

In chapter two, I describe how we can use our minds as an ally in our efforts to get the most out of each day. Together, we will consider the importance of an ever-expanding mind—one that craves and consistently seeks new information. We will also examine the health benefits of confidence, gratitude, optimism, and self-esteem.

Bring Out the Best in Others

Fred Rogers, the television host of *Mr. Rogers' Neighborhood*, once said, "We live in a world in which we need to share responsibility. It's easy to say, 'It's not my child, not my community, not my world, not my problem.' Then there are those who see the need to respond. I consider those people my heroes."[3] These words highlight the importance of service. Interestingly, from a health perspective, there is a symbiotic connection between service and health. There are a growing number of studies which suggest that helping helps the helper.

In chapter three, I define service as a personally satisfying, meaningful, and pleasurable experience in which information, skills, support, or resources are freely offered with the intent of enhancing the life of another person. This definition identifies four key components of the helping process: (1) it is personally meaningful; (2) it involves offering something; (3) its goal is to meet a need; and (4) it is freely offered.

As you read this chapter, you will develop a personal blueprint for investing in the lives of those you care about.

Eat Mindfully

Chapter four is intentionally designed to avoid the automatic negative reaction often elicited by the word "diet." The focus is on eating rather than a list of restrictions and limitations, with the primary goal of making mealtime a positive, satisfying, mindful experience.

In this chapter, you are encouraged to eat *better carbohydrates, better fats,* and *better proteins.* You will also learn to care for your own body by paying attention to important internal cues. The result is not only a personalized eating plan, but also a plan for eating that is simple and sustainable.

Exercise Faithfully

There is overwhelming evidence linking physical activity with health. A U.S. Surgeon General report states that exercise is associated with lower mortality rates, decreased risk of cardiovascular disease, lower blood pressure, decreased risk of colon cancer, and decreased risk of diabetes. In addition, individuals who exercise experience less depression and anxiety.[4]

With these findings in mind, in chapter five, I provide a detailed roadmap for developing a personalized fitness plan. As part of this process, you will learn to keep an exercise log and set exercise goals. By using these resources, you can integrate healthy activity into your daily life.

Find Peace and Relaxation

Without a doubt, stress is one of the key factors contributing to ill health in the modern world. It is easy to become overwhelmed by the many demands we face. Projects at work, family disputes, and financial pressures all take their toll. Researchers have linked stress to infectious illness, overall decline in the aged, cardiovascular disease, stroke, and sleep disorders. While it would be an exaggeration to claim that stress *causes* these illnesses, it clearly can decrease the overall quality of our lives and rob us of our joy.

I have written chapter six to help us transcend this threat to our well-being. In its pages, we will learn to calm our minds and bodies. We will also learn about the health benefits of relaxation.

Connect with the Creator

The scientific community has largely ignored the role of spirituality in health, causing Harold Koenig, a pioneer in research on religion and health, to call this area of study "medicine's last great frontier."[5] Over the past several years, however, a number of scholars have begun exploring this frontier and they have made some rather interesting discoveries. Their research links faith to a number of important health-related outcomes, including longevity, blood pressure, satisfaction, and joy.

Based on this research, chapter seven looks at the connection between faith and well-being. In this chapter, writing from a Christian perspective, I describe spirituality as a dynamic, living process involving the interaction of four dimensions of the faith journey—*contemplation, connection, expression, and integration.* With this description as a backdrop, you will have the opportunity to develop a plan designed to enhance your own spirituality.

In the remainder of this book, I will encourage you to mindfully and purposefully nurture these seven essentials. As you integrate them into your day, I hope you will observe what happens in your heart and mind. When you stop what you are doing in order to listen to a friend, how is your life altered? When you spend your Saturday at a soup kitchen, what is the impact? When you eat mindfully and exercise faithfully, is there a noticeable difference in your energy level? Does change in one area lead to change in another? I hope you will pause to savor the journey, enjoy the process, and observe its impact on your energy and mood.

Pause Points

When it comes to living well and getting the most out of each day, knowing what is beneficial is only the beginning. It is one thing to understand what is healthy but quite another thing to live a healthy lifestyle. So, in addition to knowing the essentials, we also need to know how to assimilate them into our lives.

I have developed a process for integrating healthy practices into our daily experience called *Pause Points*. This process is a dynamic, experiential, goal-directed approach to life consisting of moments in which we slow our pace and intentionally *reflect, dream, plan, connect,* and *experience* a new mindful journey.

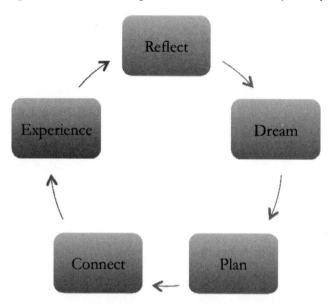

Two of the most memorable experiences of my life were the births of my children. Watching their first breaths was an awe-inspiring miracle that brought a flood of emotion. Shortly after each child arrived, my older friends reminded me the years of having a young child at home would be gone before I knew it. With the typical ignorance of youth, I did not fully comprehend the truth of these words. Now with one child in college and another in graduate school, I can say with certainty the time you have with your kids living at home passes in a heartbeat.

When viewing life through a rearview mirror, it all seems to pass so quickly. We move seamlessly from one experience or milestone to the next without pausing. One minute we are graduating from college; the next we are paying for our kids to attend.

But there is an alternative—we can slow things down and incorporate moments of reflection and redirection. Healthy living requires us to interrupt the harried pace we so naturally keep. It is a journey punctuated by frequent Pause Point moments in which we reflect, dream, plan, connect, and experience a new direction.

Reflect

All Pause Points begin with reflection—an open, honest look at our starting point at any given moment in time. These contemplative moments are created when we slow our pace and look inward, asking ourselves important questions like: What is going on with me right now? What is going well? How did I get in this particular situation? What am I feeling? How am I doing? This initial step in the Pause Point process is our mental, emotional, physical, and spiritual GPS. When we pause to reflect, we are identifying the thoughts, feelings, and behaviors that have a direct impact on our sense of meaning, satisfaction, and happiness.

At times, this reflection is stimulated by events that demand our full attention. Recently my friend Mary found herself tethered to a hospital wall by an oxygen mask. Her decades-long smoking habit was taking its toll, and this brush with mortality helped her realize she would require oxygen for the rest of her life if she did not make significant changes.

Other Pause Points are barely noticeable, often sparked by a desire to open new horizons and seek greater possibilities. Tim, another friend, began exercising after his first child was born as one way of building health into his now fuller life (read more of his story in chapter five).

By reading this book and examining your health and well-being, you are initiating a transformational journey. Your Pause Point has already begun. As you read on, I will ask you to identify weaknesses and celebrate strengths. This process of reflection and self-awareness is the fundamental beginning point of a healthy life.

As you initiate your Pause Point experience, be sure to open your heart and mind to the good you discover in yourself and your situation. One of the keys to health is slowing down and taking the time to reflect on what is going well. Barbara Fredrickson, author of the book *Positivity,* encourages her readers to ask the question, "What is right in my life right now?"[6] I suggest you spend the next few minutes considering this question. What is right at work? What is going well in your relationships? What are you grateful for? What amuses or inspires? What takes your breath away? Take time to savor all that is good.

Be as specific as possible, identifying in detail the events that capture your imagination and lift your spirit. Rewind your life and review the past few days, intentionally recalling experiences that had a positive impact. Remember who was there, what you were doing, and how you felt. Do not over-analyze or try to explain; simply appreciate what is right in your life. You may even wish to record some of your thoughts and feelings in a journal. Focus on how the experience of reflecting on the good in your life makes you feel. Does it bring a smile to your face, a tear of inspiration to your eye, or energy to your day? Allow this mental exercise to change the trajectory of your life, even if just for a brief moment.

If you find this exercise to be a negative experience because you do not believe there is much to celebrate, let me suggest that you passively disregard these negative thoughts (see chapter two) and refocus on what is right, no matter how small. I will be the first to acknowledge we can all identify plenty that is wrong, but try to push the negative aspects to the background and focus on the small things that bring a bit of sunlight to your day. Like any other skill, it takes time and practice to become aware of what is good.

Dream

Reflection often creates a desire for something new, something better, or something different. When we pause to consider our current state, we frequently identify things we would like to improve or change (that is one reason why honest reflection is so often avoided). We may discover that others find us irritable, our clothes are shrinking, or we spend too much time on the couch. Many of us know from our own experience there is a gap—if not a canyon—between our real self and our ideal self.

So how do we respond to this gap? I suggest we *dream*.

Close your eyes and see yourself in an aerobics class or losing ten pounds. Imagine a better tomorrow with your spouse. Dream about arriving at a new place in your journey—a place where you find harmony and peace.

In a fascinating experiment, social scientist Laura King explored the health benefits associated with recording life goals. She asked college students to write about their "best possible selves in the future" for twenty minutes on four consecutive days. During these writing sessions, the participants were given the following instructions:

> *Think about your life in the future. Imagine that everything has gone as well as it possibly could. You have worked hard and succeeded at accomplishing all of your life goals. Think of this as the realization of all of your life dreams. Now, write about what you imagined.*

Based on this experiment, King concluded that "writing about one's life goals was associated with feeling less upset, more happy, and getting sick less often." Her data support the hypothesis that there is a link between setting goals and getting the most out of each day.[7]

In the pages that follow, I will encourage you to create your own goals. These goals will describe a better, more idyllic future for you physically, socially, emotionally, intellectually, and spiritually. They will represent your dreams.

The goals you create should reflect what you value the most. When your goals represent things you care about, you are more inclined to commit to them and pursue them with fervor. If family and friends are

Goals
• Meaningful
• Challenging
• Positive

important to you, be sure to include them in your priorities. If you find meaning in helping the disadvantaged, make that front and center. The purpose of setting goals is to focus your time and effort on what is most meaningful to you.

Also, challenge yourself by setting your standards high. Because each of us has different talents and abilities, what is challenging to one individual may be quite easy to another. Running a 5K race is a significant stretch for some, but it is a walk in the park for others. Set difficult goals that will push you to experience a healthier mind and body.

One other thing: state your goals in positive terms. A well-articulated goal is expressed in terms of what is to be accomplished rather than what is to be discontinued. Let your goals describe what you wish to achieve rather than what you wish to avoid.

Goals:
O Help feed the hungry in my community
O Increase intimacy with my spouse
O Finish my college degree
O Change jobs

As you read the chapters that follow, I hope you will begin to dream of a more meaningful future. This Pause Point exercise can become a powerful tool for healthy change.

Plan

Every journey has a beginning, middle, and end. When it comes to our health, awareness (reflect) is the beginning of our journey, goal setting (dream) defines the endpoint, and planning describes the road we travel to reach the journey's end.

I prefer to think of a plan as a checklist populated with the tasks required to reach a desired objective. For example, if your goal is to increase intimacy with your spouse, your plan might include establishing a date night, planning a second honeymoon, meeting for lunch, and attending a marriage enrichment seminar. Each of these tasks is designed to move you closer to your goal of greater intimacy.

Plan: Increase intimacy with my spouse
○ Establish a date night
○ Plan a second honeymoon
○ Meet for lunch
○ Attend a marriage enrichment seminar

In the pages that follow, as you develop your personalized approach to health and well-being, I will encourage you to develop plans for reaching your goals. These plans are vital to the Pause Point process. They serve as your daily reminder of what is healthy, keeping you focused and heading in the right direction.

Connect

At a recent seminar, one of the participants said he was a great starter but a poor finisher. His enthusiasm would often quickly fade after beginning a task with great energy and vision. He went on to say this was a family trait that had repeated itself over a number of generations. He wanted to know what would help him move beyond this pattern because it was frustrating him, limiting his ability to succeed, and stealing his joy.

I pointed out his Pause Point had already begun. In fact, he was well down the road because he was already aware finishing was an issue. I suggested to him the next step might be to tell others about this issue in his life. By sharing his story, I believed he would find the support and encouragement necessary to make the changes he desired.

If well-being is anything, it is a team sport. Whether we are striving to strengthen our relationships, manage stress, or alter our eating pattern, our connections with others are a valuable resource. The journey is sweeter when it is shared with those who want the best for us. If others are walking with us, they can celebrate our victories and share our struggles.

In a frequently cited study, Christopher Langston examines how we can capitalize on the positive moments we experience during our day. He suggests we can augment and extend the good that occurs in our life by sharing it with others.[8] When we tell others about our good fortune, we are expanding the impact of that good news. Our successes are reinforced when they are shared.

Has this been your experience? Do you enjoy telling others about the tender moments with your kids? When you tell your roommate about an A on a difficult exam, are the positive feelings accentuated and extended? Sweet moments are made even sweeter when you let others know.

Find people who want to live well and join them. It need not be formal or rigidly structured; in fact, make it an integrated piece of your current, ongoing relationships. Simply begin to share with those around you the steps you are taking to live a better, healthier life. Also, begin listening to others as they share all that is good in their lives. There is a reciprocity and mutuality inherent in health. Make it natural and unforced—a normal component of your daily interactions.

Experience

The critical, final piece of the Pause Point process is our moment-to-moment experience. It pulls everything together into an integrated whole. The motivation for pausing to *reflect* is to live better in the moment. We *dream* to seize the day. We *plan* so we can live the best possible life. We *connect* to enrich the here and now. By living mindfully and purposefully in the present moment, we enhance our well-being today and ensure a better, more fulfilling tomorrow.

As you read on, I hope you begin to notice and experience all that is good and healthy in your day. Savor your conversations. Enjoy lunch. Appreciate your own value. Love God. Embrace activity. Delight in helping. Discover relaxation. When you mindfully and purposely seek these essentials, an amazing transformation takes place. You begin to live your dream, seamlessly integrating it into who you are.

Quick Start Routines

I recently purchased a smart phone without a real understanding of why it received its name. Now I know—you have to be a genius to figure out how it works. The manual is thicker than some college textbooks and is certainly harder to understand. Fortunately, the phone came with a "Quick Start Guide" containing basic instructions and a picture of the phone with each button appropriately labeled. Without this guide, I would still be learning how to turn it on and off.

I have applied this quick start idea to the concepts in this book. At the end of each chapter, I ask you to create a Quick Start Routine designed to help you get off on the right foot. These routines consist of valued actions performed at regular intervals.[9]

You probably already have some important routines in your life. I know I do. As I write these words, I am participating in one of my routines; I wake up early most Saturday mornings to work on this book.

What are some routines already punctuating your life, helping you get the most out of each day? Pause here for a moment to identify them, and write them down.

Healthy Routines

○

○

○

○

Routines, and our efforts to improve them, are important to our health. They provide a consistent structure in which to experience the healthy change we desire. As you work through the exercises in this book, the routines you create can become effective tools for reaching your goals.

SEVEN ESSENTIALS
OF
HEALTH AND WELL-BEING

One

Love the Ones You're With

For without friends no one would choose to live,
though he had all other goods.
—Aristotle

Have you observed a connection between your relationships and your well-being? On days when all is well in your social network, are you more energetic and focused? Conversely, when there is conflict with those you care about, is life more challenging?

Take a minute to think back over the past few days, months, or even years to determine if your relational health and your physical health are connected. Remember your last illness; was it associated with a significant change in your support system? Has the state of your relationships ever influenced your effectiveness at work? Has your happiness, peace, and satisfaction ever been affected by what was happening in your friendships?

Try to identify specific situations, both good and bad, and recall what was going on in your interactions with family and friends.

Relationships, Health, and Well Being

When a relationship does not work out, it is common to hear the words, "I'm heartbroken." If you have ever had a relationship that ended in disappointment, maybe you have said these very words. The irony is this phrase describes an actual physical reality; there is a very real connection between relational health and physical health.

In an article published in the medical journal, *Circulation,* Alan Rozanski describes a link between social interactions and the development of heart disease. After reviewing a large number of studies, he concludes that individuals with few social contacts are more likely to develop blockages in their coronary arteries (i.e., heart disease). Interestingly, he also notes that following an initial heart attack, individuals who have supportive relationships are less likely to have a second heart attack.[1] These findings are echoed in a study conducted by C. Welin. In his study, Welin reports that a lack of social support is associated with an increased risk of fatal heart attacks in patients who have suffered a prior heart attack.[2] These studies suggest that healthy relationships reduce the risk and impact of heart disease.

Janice Kiecolt-Glaser, a highly regarded scholar, has examined the association between our immune system and a variety of psychological factors. In her published studies, she notes that those who are having relational difficulties have higher rates of medical problems, including higher rates of death from infectious diseases and up to six times as many deaths from pneumonia.[3] Her research suggests the function of our immune system is impaired by relational strife.

There is also a close connection between our social network and our mental health. Ichiro Kawachi and Lisa Berkman, in their research, note that a smaller social network, fewer close relationships, and lower perceived adequacy of social support are all connected with depression. Depression is also associated with a lack of emotional support during childhood from parents or caregivers. Moreover, social isolation and the loss of social ties are among the most potent predictors of depressive symptoms among the elderly.[4]

The take-home message is clear: relationships have a significant, measurable impact on physical and mental health. Healthy relationships promote healthy hearts, healthy immune systems, and healthy minds.

Healthy Connections

This research begs the question—what are the characteristics of a healthy relationship? It is intuitively obvious (and scientifically sound) that some relationships are better than others.

So, what does a healthy relationship look like? In the pages that follow, I propose that healthy relationships are created through an ongoing process that fosters *engagement, encouragement, care, communication, excitement, boundaries,* and *synergy.* When nurtured in our relationships, these characteristics produce social bonds that generate a sense of peace, harmony, and well-being.

Relationships
• Engagement
• Encouragement
• Care
• Communication
• Excitement
• Boundaries
• Synergy

Engagement

Have you ever experienced an interaction in which you were talking but nobody was listening? Perhaps a friend was texting, posting on Twitter, or just daydreaming as you told him about your day. Or maybe you were the one distracted. Arriving home, you grunted hello to your spouse, told your kids to do their homework, read while eating dinner, finished up odds and ends from work, and fell asleep watching television. You felt good because you were home all evening—but were you actually present?

In their bestselling book, *The Power of Full Engagement,* Jim Loehr and Tony Schwartz argue that success is determined more by how we manage our focus and energy than how we manage our time.[5] They suggest, in order to succeed, we must ignore distractions and pay close attention to whatever is in front of us at any given moment.

I believe this concept applies to relationships. An important key to social interactions is being fully present and 100 percent engaged.

Has this been your experience? When you are attentive and engaged, is there a noticeable change in the nature and depth of your conversations? How do you feel when others seem uninterested in what you have to say?

The next time you have a chance encounter with some friends, slow your pace, take a genuine interest in what they are saying, and see what happens; see if being engaged changes the tenor of the interaction.

Encouragement

One of the most frequently quoted experts on the nature and quality of our relationships is John Gottman. In his book *What Predicts Divorce?*, he notes that relationships with more positive than negative interactions are more satisfying and tend to last longer. According to Gottman, the ratio of positive to negative found in stable relationships is five to one; that is, those who relate well offer five positive interactions to one that is negative.[6]

Thriving relationships are built on a steady diet of positive interactions. Think of your interactions with others as deposits and withdrawals from a bank account. When you offer an encouraging word or pat on the back, you make a deposit that earns positive relational dividends. On the other side of the ledger, when you are critical or condescending, you make a withdrawal that strains your relationships.

Over the next few days, pay attention to the relational deposits and withdrawals in your significant relationships and see where you are with respect to Gottman's five-to-one ratio.

Care

I recently attended the funeral of my wife's grandfather, a husband and father of three who lived most of his adult life in a small Midwestern town. While he was a respected businessman with many professional accomplishments, during the funeral he was not remembered for what he had done professionally. Instead, he was remembered for small acts of kindness. Friends and family reminisced about the pony rides, the golf lessons, and the rides to church he so freely offered. At the end of his life, he was warmly remembered and widely praised for his caring.

Caring is a critical component of any healthy relationship. It is the glue that holds us together—the currency of a strong, thriving interpersonal economy. While it takes many forms, caring is primarily based on small acts of kindness that are freely offered without expecting anything in return.

To grow this currency, try the following exercise: ask a close friend or family member to write down four small, positive, inexpensive things you can do to show you care. While he or she makes a list, you make a list as well. On your list, write four small, positive, inexpensive things your friend or family member can do for you. Once these acts of kindness are written down, exchange lists and perform the requested acts over the next few days or weeks. As you do, monitor the effect on you, the other person, and your relationship.

Care: What can I do for you?
O
O
O
O

Initially, this exercise will likely feel contrived and awkward—most new habits do. But stick with it; over time it can become a natural part of your relational life.

This approach to demonstrating kindness is designed to eliminate some of the guesswork inherent in any relationship. We often make assumptions about what others might like, but if what we do is not perceived as caring, then it will not be received well—no matter how hard we try. Putting our preferences in writing eliminates trial and error and the need for mind reading.

If you have difficulty finding a friend or family member who is willing to do this exercise with you, or if you have difficulty asking someone to participate, you can do this exercise on your own. Simply make a list of four small, positive, inexpensive things you wish to offer to someone else, and over the next few days perform the acts of kindness you have recorded. As you do this exercise, be sure to observe its impact on you and your relationships. Do you sense a change in how others respond when you enter a room? Do you feel more connected?

Before leaving this section, let me share some thoughts about caring I have learned from my own experience. One of my favorite ways of deepening my connections with others is meditation. I pause on a regular basis to mentally rewind my life and recall meaningful social interactions. These moments of reflection are truly transformational. I feel myself being drawn to those I care about. I will often experience a sense of gratitude and well-being that draws me closer to those who mean the most to me.

If you want to try this type of meditation, find a quiet place and sit or recline in a relaxed position. Allow your breathing to be the focus of your attention. Mindfully concentrate on what it is like to simply inhale and exhale. You may wish to close your eyes. If you have a thought that draws your mind away, disregard it and reorient to your breathing. After a minute or two, allow your mind to reflect on the love, warmth, and caring you feel toward significant people in your life. Simply reflect on pleasurable interactions. It may be a casual touch, a walk in the park, a pleasant conversation, a loving caress, or a kind word. Dwell on these meaningful moments and relive their impact. As you do this exercise, you may experience feelings of tenderness, kindness, love, caring, contentment, or joy. Savor these memories, reliving them in great detail.

I have integrated this type of meditation into my daily routine and will frequently begin my morning by reflecting on the positive interactions in my life. I have discovered it helps me build healthy, strong, caring connections. By remembering a kind word from my spouse, a call from my son or daughter, or a heartfelt "thank you" from a colleague, I am energized and my well-being is enhanced. The positive emotions I feel animate my life, adding energy to my day. As a result of these moments of reflection, I become more attuned to the meaningful social interactions occurring each day, and I feel more connected to the people crossing my path.

Communication

Communication is at the very core of our being; we love to share our stories. By talking and listening, we build bonds that sweeten success and make misfortune a bit more bearable. It seems all of life, the good and bad, is better when shared.

Meaningful dialogue is dependent on our willingness to focus our attention outside of ourselves and understand the thoughts, dreams, and experiences of others. In his book *The Road Less Traveled*, M. Scott Peck calls this process *bracketing*. He writes, "An essential part of true listening is the discipline of bracketing, the temporary giving up or setting aside of one's own prejudices, frames of reference and desires so as to experience as far as possible the speaker's world from the inside, stepping inside his or her shoes" (p. 127).[7]

This ability to enter the world of another is essential to successful communication. If we desire to understand the thoughts, desires, and dreams of others, we must be willing to suspend our own agenda and listen intently. Meaningful communication begins with careful listening.

Meaningful dialogue also requires self-awareness. The better we know ourselves, the better we are able to share what is on our hearts. It may seem odd we would need to be encouraged to get to know ourselves better. But in our action-oriented society, there is little premium placed on silence and introspection.

Consider your own experience: How much of your day is spent just listening to yourself, eavesdropping on your own inner dialogue? Are you constantly in motion, or do you take time for reflection?

Communication is based on careful listening. As we listen to ourselves and grow in understanding of our own inner world, we are better able to share with others what is meaningful to us. As we listen to others, we enter their world and gain insight into their beliefs and perspectives. While talking is common, communication based on listening is quite rare.

Excitement

While I am ashamed to admit it, I own a wiener dog. It was not my idea, but I have a nine-pound (actually ten, but he is sensitive about his weight), brown-eyed, black miniature dachshund. This dog has a laundry list of annoying habits. He gets up too early, leaves deposits on the carpet, and barks incessantly, irritating anyone who dares enter his territory. He does, however, have at least one endearing quality; he is always excited to see me. When I arrive home after work, you would think I was a T-bone steak. Running, jumping, licking, and barking, he instantly changes from a docile animal resting on his cushion to an exuberantly animated purveyor of the message, "Welcome home!"

I wonder what would happen in our relationships if we consistently greeted friends and family with the attention and excitement offered by my dog (minus the licking and jumping of course). If we communicated, "I'm glad to see you!" with our eye contact, mood, and words, would we not build immensely rewarding bonds? Excitement to see others is an acknowledgment of their importance, and it communicates we value them and enjoy having them around.

Shelly Gable, in her research on the sharing of positive experiences, discovered relationships are affected by how we respond when good news is shared.[8] When we respond with interest and enthusiasm, our connections with others are strengthened and our positive experiences are enhanced. By celebrating with others, we build strong interpersonal bonds.

You may wish to give this a try. The next time someone shares a positive life event with you, focus your attention, share the excitement, and ask questions designed to learn more. Listen to the story, and join in the celebration. Then, observe the impact on you and those around you.

Boundaries

I heard a story, many years ago, about a large, grassy elementary school playground encircled by a chain-link fence. Each day, during recess, children would play games in the enclosed playground. One day, school officials decided the play area looked too much like a prison exercise yard and they removed the fence. Much to everyone's surprise, the children no longer used the entire play area for their recess games; instead, they stayed close to the building and away from the boundary where the fence had once stood. Seemingly, the fence had provided a sense of safety and security, giving the children freedom to explore and play.

Like a playground fence, thriving relationships have clear boundaries defining what is and is not appropriate. These boundaries provide safety and they structure our interactions with each other.

We set relational boundaries by saying no: "No, that's not appropriate," or "No, I can't do that," or "No, that's not acceptable to me." When we say no, we are telling others where we stand and clarifying the rules that define our interactions.

While setting boundaries may seem rather simple, in practice it is often quite difficult, because what is appropriate in one relationship is not necessarily appropriate in another. Setting limits is also difficult because our needs change. Changing situations in our relationships and in ourselves require us to adjust the boundaries we set. Finally, and probably most importantly, good limits are hard to set because we are often confused about what we want. We have mixed feelings, and mixed feelings result in mixed messages (We say no with our mouth, but other things about us, including our actions, say yes).

With these difficulties in mind, I have developed a few guidelines for establishing relational boundaries.

First, while certain boundaries should be inflexible (for instance, abusive behavior is never justified), most boundaries should have a degree of flexibility. You may be too tired to jog with a friend today, but tomorrow may be fine. You may not want to discuss a personal matter at this moment, but you may change your mind in a few hours. Flexible boundaries allow a relationship to adjust to changing needs.

Clarity is also important; while it is true that most limits require flexibility, flexibility is not synonymous with ambiguity. A limit can be flexible and changing over time, yet clear at any given point in time. The fence posts move, but they are easily identifiable. Clarity of limits is critical to the development of safe relational space. When we know the limits of a relationship, we feel more comfortable and safe in that relationship.

Another guideline to consider is not too many, not too few. Too many boundaries stifle a relationship. A person who erects multiple boundaries is standoffish, building walls that create distance and separation. If your answer is always no, ultimately you will have no relationships. Conversely, the absence of boundaries is equally unhealthy. If you set too few limits, no one knows where you stand. Like a chameleon, you change your color from one minute to the next and become difficult to predict. Healthy relationships are based on a proper balance between too many and too few limits.

One final note on boundaries—in a healthy relationship, *both* parties respect limits. If a friend, colleague, or family member says no, the limit is honored. The *sine qua non* of a safe relationship is a mutual understanding and respect for personal boundaries.

Synergy

Another quality of healthy social connections is synergy. In a growing relationship, both parties win; in fact, not only does each person win, each person is better because he or she has met the other. Together, they explore life goals, ambitions, and dreams—partners in facing the joys and the challenges of life.

One man I know quit his job after he and his wife had their first child. He did this in order to care for their baby while his wife completed medical residency. The result? Both the husband and wife are invigorated. The stay-at-home dad had been in a less-than-fulfilling job; now, when he is not caring for the needs of their child, he is able to pursue avocational interests he finds rewarding. At the same time, his wife is achieving meaningful goals as she pursues her career in medicine. Both are thriving in their newly defined roles.

Another couple I know find synergy as they pursue mutual dreams; he is an artist, and she is an accomplished business manager. While he is creating, she is promoting, marketing, and keeping the books. Their individual success and satisfaction is exponentially better because they are together.

Who in your world shares your dreams, making you better? Whose life is enriched by your presence?

Your health and well-being is enhanced by mutually beneficial relationships—the ones that bring out the very best in you.

Engagement, encouragement, care, communication, excitement, boundaries, and *synergy* are all hallmarks of healthy, growing connections with others. Relationships possessing these qualities fill our lives with mutual, health-giving support.

Pause Points

With these characteristics of a healthy relationship in mind, pause for a minute to consider your own life, health, and social connections.

Reflect

A good place to begin is your most-treasured relationships. Identify the individuals who mean the most to you. They may be friends, family members, mentors, or respected colleagues. Focus your attention on a particularly positive relationship, reflecting on the factors that make this relationship so special. What does this person do or say? What one word would you use to describe the relationship? When you are around this person, how do you feel? Consider how your life is better because this individual has crossed your path.

I have a dear friend I met in college; we share a bond that is difficult to explain. He is genuine and refreshingly authentic. When we talk, he is fully engaged, setting aside his own thoughts and feelings in order to listen. He is the person I contact when I am considering a complex question or making a key life transition. There is a mutual respect and common desire to bring out the best in each other. We share successes and commiserate over challenges.

Continue this time of reflection by shifting your attention to the moment-to-moment, positive interpersonal interactions that are part of your day. Begin by thinking back to a specific, especially meaningful interaction—one that left you feeling good. Replay the interaction in your mind, asking yourself what made it so meaningful? What did the other person do or say that influenced how you felt? Repeat this process with one or two additional encounters. These interactions need not be long or involved; in fact, they could be chance meetings lasting only a brief moment. The importance lies not in the duration but in the positive impact.

As you reflect on your connections with others, be sure to highlight what is good and savor the interpersonal moments that mean the most to you. Allow the positive in your relationships to change the trajectory of your day.

Also, allow what you observe to become a catalyst for change. Any new awareness can be the inspiration for a personal transformation. If you find your friendships lack good boundaries or your marriage needs more excitement, let these insights motivate you to set a different course. Resolve to explore new and exciting territory.

Dream

Honest reflection often creates a desire for change. When we take an inventory of our current state (reflection), we are frequently left wanting more.

Borrowing from and adapting the work of King, whose research I cited earlier,[9] consider the following mental exercise:

Think about your life in the future. Imagine that everything has gone as well as it possibly could in your relationships. You have worked hard and succeeded at deepening your connection with others. You have reached your best-imagined future with the people in your life. Now create a clear mental image of a personalized, highly desired future that is filled with healthy, life-giving relationships.

After you have spent some time imagining a better future in your relationships, take a moment to describe this future in writing by setting challenging, positive, meaningful, and exciting goals. These goals provide a snapshot of a desired destination. At this point, try not to be too critical of the ideas that come to mind. Simply record what you imagined as you thought about a better future for your relationships.

I have provided an example of some relational goals, as well as space for you to record some of your own.

Goals:

O Widen my circle of friends

O Communicate better with my spouse

O A closer connection with my kids

O

Goals:

O

O

O

O

Plan

With your dreams in mind and your goals in hand, the next Pause Point task is making a plan. A workable plan is a checklist of items detailing what needs to be accomplished in order to reach a particular goal.

Take a minute to review my sample plan; then devise a plan for one of your goals.

Plan: A closer connection with my kids
O Establish a regular kids' night out
O Be home in the evening most days
O Be engaged when with my kids
O

Plan:
O
O
O
O

Connect

Now that you are well along in this Pause Point process, begin to share this part of your journey with others. It does not have to be forced or awkward. You do not have to make an appointment, nor do you have to do it all at once. Simply let others know what you are doing. Tell your spouse you are trying to be more attentive to your children when you come home from work. Ask a friend how he or she sets good boundaries. Share with others so they can support your dream of better, healthier relationships.

Seek the company of those who resonate with your desire to connect more meaningfully. Look for individuals who will engage you, encourage you, care for you, listen to you, enjoy being with you, and respect your boundaries. These connections will enrich your life and enhance your health.

Experience

What remains is the best part, bringing your dreams to life.

The next time you are with friends, become mindful of what is going on in that moment in time and purposely connect with them, even if it is a ten-second impromptu meeting in an elevator. Focus and listen intently to what they are saying. Ask questions and learn about their current interests. Intentionally slow down and become aware of the entire experience, living fully in the moment.

As you travel through life, consciously choose the less-travelled path that leads to better health. Initially, it may seem artificial or mechanical. The first time you call your spouse in the middle of the day, write a note to a friend, send an e-mail to a colleague, or invite a college buddy to lunch, you might feel this new behavior is odd or out of character. Do not be discouraged. Give it time, and soon it will become as natural as breathing or walking.

When we meaningfully interact with others, we are transformed. While the outcome is better health, savoring the journey is the best part.

Quick Start Routine

It is Thursday, and it is taco night at Mom and Dad Harker's house in middle America. Any family members who happen to be in town, whether they live nearby or are visiting from a thousand miles away, participate in this important family event. A short drive is made to a local restaurant to buy the hard-shell, meat-filled, cheese-laden tacos. While seemingly mundane, this weekly experience provides the perfect structure for important family dialogue and relationship building. It is a scheduled interpersonal experience (routine), providing the perfect venue for deepening the inter-relatedness that is essential to health.

To add to the relationships in your life, consider starting some routines of your own. As discussed in an earlier section, a routine is a regularly scheduled, highly valued activity. What would a healthy relational routine look like for you? Could it be a date night or going to the movies every Saturday with your kids? Perhaps it is meeting with a group to promote a cause or enjoying a hobby that brings together individuals with similar interests.

It need not be too difficult. A routine can be as simple as hugging your spouse when she arrives home or meeting friends for coffee on Friday mornings. It does not have to be tedious or time-consuming to be valuable. The best routines are the ones that are meaningful and help you reach your goals.

Two

Fill Your Mind with the Best

*Did you ever stop to think
and forget to start again?*
—Winnie-the-Pooh (A. A. Milne)

A few years ago, I ran across a rather morbid, but strangely intriguing website called *Death Clock* (www.deathclock.com). This site uses information like date of birth, sex, smoking habits, body mass index (see chapter four), and "mode" to predict a person's date of death. The choices in the drop-down menu for mode include "normal," "optimistic," "pessimistic," and "sadistic." Depending on which mode is selected, there are significant changes in the predicted date of death.

For instance, when I input my data and select "pessimistic," the site predicts my death will occur on April 1, 2017. In contrast, if I select "optimistic" the site extends my life by thirty-seven years, predicting I will die on June 16, 2054. By simply switching from "pessimistic" to "optimistic," I gain almost four decades of life. (Eeyore, eat your heart out!)

While it is unlikely that optimists will live decades longer than pessimists, there is good data supporting a connection between a positive outlook on life and wellness. Optimism is linked to well-being, less frequent doctor visits, longer survival time following a heart attack, greater immune function, successful completion of rehabilitation programs, and longevity. It decreases the likelihood of illness, minimizes the severity of illness, speeds recovery, and makes relapses less likely.[1] In short, optimism is an important indicator of health.

Research in the social and physical sciences consistently demonstrates that mental processes are important for individuals coping with serious illnesses like cancer, AIDS, and coronary artery disease. There is also a mental component to willingness to seek medical care, preparation for medical procedures, compliance with medical care, and use of alcohol and drugs.[2] Researchers are reporting that mental life and physical health are intertwined in complex ways.

In this chapter, we take a look at the interface between our mental life and our health. As we will see, health is associated with an expanding mind—one that craves and consistently seeks new information from a wide variety of sources. We will also learn about the connection between self-esteem, gratitude, confidence, optimism, and mental and physical well-being.

An Expanding Mind

The phrase "use it or lose it" is frequently employed to describe muscle loss due to inactivity. If we do not use a particular muscle, it will shrink in size and weaken. This is most dramatically seen if we fracture a bone and are required to wear a cast. The cast prevents muscle use, which ultimately results in muscle loss.

Even if we have never worn a cast, all of us have lost abilities due to lack of use. For example, as the years pass, most of us no longer have the strength, endurance, or flexibility we once had. While some of this decline is the inevitable companion of aging, some of it is related to changes in behavior. Most of us do not exercise enough or stretch enough to maintain our physical exercise capacity. If we are not using it, we are losing it.

This atrophy due to inactivity is not limited to physical strength; it applies to our minds as well. Based on his research, Gary Small, the director of the UCLA Center on Aging, concludes that "mental stimulation, or exerting our brains in various ways intellectually, may tone up our memory performance, protect us from future decline in brain function, and may even lead to new brain cell growth in the future" (p. 87).[3] Small's research suggests that when we engage our minds and actively process the information gathered by our senses, we are exercising our minds and making an important contribution to our health.

I have observed firsthand the lifelong benefits of intellectual activity and curiosity. My parents could be the poster children for healthy mental activity; on a daily basis, they are working on a Sudoku puzzle, completing a crossword puzzle, or reading a book. By consistently engaging in stimulating intellectual tasks, they challenge their minds and expand their mental horizons.

While we may grow weary of preschoolers who incessantly ask questions, it is their curiosity that drives their growth and development. They engage their world with unquenchable interest—a dry sponge in a rich environment filled with learning opportunities. If we can imitate this curiosity, we will live inspired lives, actively growing each day.

To help broaden your world, consider the following list of *simple ways to expand your mind.*

Simple Ways to Expand Your Mind	
Read	Keep a journal
Try a new food	Camp out
Take a class	Write a poem
Go for a walk	Join a fitness center
Turn off the TV	Chew your food
Write an editorial	Go skiing
Go swimming	Watch a documentary

Go to a movie	Go to the park
Do a crossword puzzle	Build a model airplane
Read to someone else	Take the stairs
Write a letter	Travel somewhere new
Get a massage	Change the oil in your car
Take a friend to lunch	Volunteer
Go for a drive	Fix something
Teach a class	Run a race
Savor a food	Plant a garden
Smell a flower	Plan a party
Hand wash your car	Solve a math problem
E-mail	Learn a new language
Make a list	Memorize a Bible verse
Go on a hike	Call a friend
Cross-train	Meditate
Read the newspaper	Savor a sunset
Go for a bike ride	Tell a joke
Dance	Go fishing
Listen to a book on tape	Perform an act of kindness
Make a clay model	Create a website
Paint a picture	Go to a museum
Play a board game	Learn a new piece of software
Take a different route to work	Go to a theme park
Walk a dog	*Read*

As you may have noticed, this list begins with the suggestion "*read*" and ends with the same suggestion. This is not an oversight; reading is essential to the development of a healthy mind. The other suggestions are important, but reading is indispensable. Read fiction, non-fiction, inspirational, classics, how-to, and advice books. Read magazines, journals, newspapers, and Internet sources. Open your mind to words and discover where the journey leads.

Pause Points

Before leaving this section, pause to celebrate your successes, open your mind, and where needed, plot a new course designed to fill your mind with the best.

Reflect

Begin by taking a mental inventory of the events and situations currently capturing your imagination. It may be a project at work, a relationship you are cultivating, or a trip you are planning. Try not to make this too scripted or difficult; simply pause to reflect on what is grabbing and holding your attention.

These moments of heightened mental activity need not all be intellectual pursuits like reading a textbook or solving a puzzle. Simple things, such as a pristine beach or a beautiful trail in the local park, can completely capture our imagination. As you reflect on these health-giving, mind-expanding moments, savor the good feelings that naturally follow; pause to appreciate them.

Use this time of reflection as a catalyst for building a greater appreciation for who you are. Build on your mind's natural craving for what is interesting and novel, embracing the process of meaningful connections with the events, people, and situations in your day.

Dream

Continue this Pause Point process by imagining a future filled with unique activities and mind-expanding experiences. Consider what you might do tomorrow or over the next few days that would capture your imagination. Is there something you would like to understand more fully? Are there places you have never been? Is there an author who intrigues you?

As you consider these questions, begin setting goals designed to help you reach your desired future. At this point, try not to dwell too long on any one goal—be open to almost anything. Simply write down the goals that come to mind. I have provided an example to stimulate your thinking. Remember, you are setting goals that will encourage curiosity, stimulate creativity, and engage your mind.

Goals:
O Travel more widely
O Learn more about computers
O Plant a garden
O Finish my college degree

Goals:
O
O
O
O

Plan

Just as you did in the prior chapter, select one of your goals and develop a plan to reach that goal. I have provided an example for you to consider. After reviewing this example, develop a plan that fits your needs and situation.

Plan: Learn more about computers
O Enroll in a computer course
O Read a book about computers
O Build a computer
O

Plan:
O
O
O
O

Connect

As you broaden your horizons and try new experiences, start sharing this piece of your journey with others. Whether it is cooking, sailing, jogging, or camping, allow others to know where your passions lie. You might even consider joining a club or organization of like-minded individuals who share your interests. Regardless of how you do it, intentionally create a fertile environment of mind-expanding connections.

Listen intently to what others are saying and discover what is capturing their imagination. Ask your friends, colleagues, neighbors, or even acquaintances, "What's new?" It is often in a conversation that you will gain a new perspective on a problem, experience a moment of creative inspiration, or learn a new bit of information.

Experience

With the new insights you have gained by reflecting, dreaming, planning, and connecting, begin to experience your world differently. Let mind-broadening curiosity be the centerpiece of your day. Spend that extra minute to listen to your spouse. Look upon your toddler as if it were the first time. As you drive to work, be more aware. Do not miss a beautiful sunrise, a flowering tree, or a cloudless, blue sky. Exercise your mind by reading a book or enrolling in a class. Expand your horizons, living mindfully aware of the richness that is all around.

Habitual Thoughts

While an expanding mind is undoubtedly important, habitual thoughts are also significant. These thoughts are our constant companions—a steady stream of mental activity profoundly influencing our experience and well-being.

Thinking, thinking, thinking —we are always thinking. Every waking moment our minds are generating an endless stream of ideas, questions, criticisms, hopes, dreams, and plans. Most of this thinking occurs automatically without any real awareness on our part. Like the hum of a florescent light, thoughts are a constant noise in the background of our minds.

Habitual thoughts ...

- Constant
- Hidden
- Powerful
- Believed without question
- Universally applied
- Learned from experience
- Often not based on data

But do not underestimate their influence. Although they are in the background, habitual thoughts have a profound impact on our feelings and actions. They have a great deal to do with how we experience life, forming a scaffold for how we perceive our current situation and our future. If in our thoughts we are self-critical, if we view our situation as hopeless, or if we believe our future is bleak, it is likely we will experience discouragement and have trouble finding the initiative to be an active participant in life. Conversely, if we are more hopeful in our inner dialogue, believing we are capable and feeling good about our circumstances, we are likely to experience more energy and face problems with greater confidence. These automatic, habitual thoughts are silent yet mighty.

We usually accept these thoughts as valid and true, regardless of the evidence. Based on the overall pattern of our life experiences, we have come to think about our situation, our future, and ourselves in a fixed way. We rarely take the time to evaluate or challenge these conclusions. These silent messages are given the benefit of the doubt and accepted without question, regardless of the facts.

Also, automatic, habitual thoughts are remarkably stable. While your experiences may change, your thoughts will stubbornly stay the same. For example, if one of your consistent automatic thoughts is, "I can't handle it," this thought will occur whether or not you have the skill, ability, and resources to handle a particular situation. Regardless of the success you may experience, it will be difficult to escape this negative mantra.

Each of us has our own personal collection of automatic, habitual thoughts. They are constant, powerful, hidden, believed without question, consistent across situations, learned as the result of prior experiences, and often not based on the objective realities of a given situation. They reside in the background, exerting great influence.

Fortunately, this is not the end of the story. Although habitual thoughts are frequently outside our awareness, with a little effort we can become more aware of their presence and make them part of our conscious mind. We can start paying attention to our inner dialogue, moving it from the background into the foreground.

Some individuals find journaling a helpful tool for heightening their awareness of habitual thoughts. Consider using a thought journal to begin recording what is going on in your life, your reaction to what is going on, and the stream of thoughts passing through your mind. Simply pause during your day to record the thoughts shaping your feelings and actions.

Thought Journal	
Events/Reactions	Thoughts
Playing with your child ... A sense of peace and satisfaction	I'm grateful. She's so beautiful. Her smile brings great joy.
The morning commute ... Helplessness, resentment, and frustration	I'm trapped in this worthless job!

Thought Journal	
Events/Reactions	**Thoughts**

As you become more aware of your thoughts, start looking for connections between your thoughts and your feelings, your thoughts and your experiences, and your thoughts and your actions. You may discover your feelings about your co-workers can be predicted from your inner dialogue about them. You may also observe that your fear about tomorrow is rooted in what you believe about the future. Your perceptions about your ability to cope with a particular problem may be contributing to your anxiety. Look for these connections and see if they help you understand yourself better.

As you become familiar with your inner world, patterns may emerge. Habitual thoughts often contain themes. Are your thoughts, for the most part, more self-critical or self-forgiving, more negative or positive, more hopeful or hopeless? Do your thoughts suggest you are a person of value, or do they imply you are powerless to do anything about your situation? Is your thinking black-and-white (everything is either perfect or perfectly miserable)? By identifying patterns in your thinking, you can gain a clearer picture of who you are.[4]

Our thoughts have a tremendous impact on how we experience life. What we believe about our situation, our future, and ourselves influences how we live, how we feel, and how we act.

As we consider the impact of our mental world on our experiences, it is worth noting that perceptions do not change facts. It is a fact that the Earth exerts a gravitational force; all thoughts to the contrary will not alter that fact. No matter how thoroughly convinced we might be that gravity does not exist, if we slip while climbing a ladder, we will certainly fall. Similarly, we can deny having high blood pressure and have all the positive thoughts in the world, but if our blood pressure is elevated, we have a problem. The emphasis here is not that our thoughts *change* the given reality of our situation; rather, our thoughts change the *impact* of that reality on our lives. It may be true you have just lost your job, but the ultimate impact on your feelings and behaviors is going to be profoundly affected by the thoughts associated with that loss. Perceptions, beliefs, thoughts, and attitudes do not change the facts of a situation; rather, they moderate a situation's impact on our experience, choices, and behaviors.

With this backdrop, consider what healthy thinking might look like, beginning with four words: *valuable, capable, blessed,* and *optimistic.*

Valuable

I'm valuable!

Do you believe this statement is true? Is your value as a human being unquestionable—intrinsic to life itself?

The vast majority of parents believe their children are priceless. A young mom may be up to her eyeballs in dirty diapers, but to her that child is still the most precious thing on Earth. The behavior of a teenager may be irascible, bordering on unredeemable; yet, his parents would give their lives to protect him from harm.

> **Healthy Thinking**
>
> - I'm valuable
> - I'm capable
> - I'm blessed
> - I'm optimistic

If we are able to internalize this sense of irrevocable parental love (self-esteem), it can contribute to our health and well-being in a number of ways. We may be more likely to avoid behaviors that have harmful effects on our health like smoking and substance abuse, while engaging in more positive self-care behaviors like exercise and seat belt use.[5] Emotionally, we may experience more happiness and less depression.[6]

When we value ourselves and treat ourselves with respect, we create a positive, healthy upward spiral.

Capable

I'm capable!

In the mid-1970s, Albert Bandura articulated a theory designed to explain human behavior (i.e., why we do what we do). One of the key components of this theory is a concept called self-efficacy.[7] At its core, self-efficacy refers to our *belief* in our ability or capacity to perform a desired action. This theory focuses on beliefs and perceptions rather than abilities and skills, hypothesizing that confidence produces behaviors that result in desired outcomes. If we are confident in our ability to reach a goal, it is more likely we will commit to that goal and will work harder to achieve it.

This hypothesis has found consistent support when studied in the context of health and the process of making health-related change. Self-efficacy is associated with smoking cessation, weight control, and exercise maintenance.[8] In a study of patients with rheumatoid arthritis, M. Brekke examined the association between self-efficacy and a variety of factors associated with this chronic, often-debilitating disease. He found that patients with a higher level of confidence (high self-efficacy) reported less pain and fatigue, while experiencing improved general health, better physical functioning, and increased vitality.[9] Similarly, in a study of college students, researchers identified a link between self-efficacy and positive health-related outcomes, including spiritual growth, physical fitness, and better nutrition.[10]

How about you? Do you feel capable? Are you confident in your ability to face challenges, or are you more tentative and cautious about your abilities?

If you are in the latter group, the good news is self-efficacy can be nurtured.[11] For example, you can build confidence by recalling past successes. Think back to the course you passed with honors or the successful work project you led. Focus on situations in which you were an active participant in reaching meaningful goals. Do not be self-critical—simply savor prior accomplishments. By recalling past achievements, you can create positive expectations regarding your ability to effect change and influence outcomes.

Nurturing Confidence
• Savor success
• Observe others
• Imagine influence
• Seek support

You can also increase your confidence by observing others.

In my job, I train resident physicians. During residency training, the primary teaching method is direct supervision in the context of ongoing patient care. The strength of this approach lies in the learning that occurs from observing experienced physicians. Not only do the resident doctors learn the details of what to do, but they also gain confidence, which enables them to practice independently once they have completed their training. They learn an "I can do that" belief (self-efficacy) by observing what more experienced physicians are able to do.

Your imagination is another effective tool for enhancing self-efficacy. When you imagine yourself reaching your goals, you boost your confidence.

The next time you are preparing a presentation for a group, imagine yourself in front of the group feeling comfortable and doing well. Then, when you actually give the presentation, see if there is an impact on your confidence and performance. Perhaps you are having difficulty dealing with a friend's behavior toward you but have not found the courage to say anything. Before moving forward, imagine yourself talking with your friend and expressing yourself clearly. When you imagine yourself being effective, you increase the likelihood of reaching your goals.

A final source for increasing self-efficacy is the influence and encouragement of others. In your life, intentionally seek out others who believe in you and support what you are doing. Develop friendships with individuals who want you to succeed, and see what happens to your confidence. Do you find you are trying new things? Are you more willing to continue at a task that in the past you would have avoided because you found it too difficult?

Never underestimate the significance of an encouraging word. The support of others is a powerful agent of change. Seek the support of others and observe what happens to your thoughts, feelings, and actions.

Blessed

I'm blessed!

One of the fascinating discoveries by researchers in the social sciences is a connection between gratitude and well-being. Evidence from this research suggests that the simple act of being thankful can change the trajectory of our lives. The object of this gratitude can be as common as the air we breathe or as unique as the third-grade teacher who pointed us in the right direction. It can be as mundane as a car starting when it is below zero or as spectacular as a picturesque view from a mountaintop. When we pause to thank God for our daily bread, we are offering gratitude to the Creator. When we tell our mentors how much we value what they are doing for us, we are expressing our appreciation for the difference they are making in our lives. When we appreciate a beautiful sunset or wonder at the expanse of the universe, we are opening ourselves up to the experience of awe. Gratitude is an awareness and expression of appreciation for what we have and what others do on our behalf.

In a series of three experimental studies, Robert Emmons explored the impact of gratitude on health and well-being. He asked his study participants to list things in their lives they were "grateful for or thankful for." He found that the individuals who made these lists felt better about their lives as a whole, were more optimistic, reported fewer physical complaints, spent more time exercising, had more positive feelings, and slept better.[12] By simply pausing to list what they were thankful for, the study participants experienced enhanced physical and mental well-being.

The way you choose to express your appreciation can take many forms.[13] If it works for you, keep a journal in which you make a list of the people and things for which you are grateful. You may find that meditation or prayer is the best way for you to express your deepest feelings of awe and wonder. You might benefit most when you make your expression of appreciation an interpersonal experience by sharing what you are thankful for with others.

There are even more ways to express thankfulness. If you are artistic, communicate your wonder through the use of acrylics or watercolors. You can sing of your appreciation for God, the beauty of nature, or the many rich blessings you have received. All of us have

Expressing Gratitude

- Journal
- Meditate
- Pray
- Share
- Paint
- Write
- Call
- Visit

people in our lives who have influenced who we are. Take the time to express your gratitude to them directly; send a letter, compose an e-mail, give them a call, or take them to lunch and let them know how much you value them.

Take the time to identify all the good in your life, and then creatively express how you feel. Change your approach occasionally so it does not become too stale or mechanical. Write your appreciation, speak it, paint it, and sometimes simply pause and linger, recognizing the richness that is life.

Optimistic

I'm optimistic!

Health is nourished by a positive, optimistic outlook on life. Those who live well anticipate the best, living life with positive expectations. They are satisfied with their current place in life or are actively doing something to change it. They find pleasure in their interactions with others and are flexible and comfortable in most situations. Even if the current day is not exactly what they had planned, they anticipate tomorrow will be a new opportunity filled with promise and hope.

This is not to deny that bad things happen, because they do. This is not to say we should smile and passively ignore the problems that come our way, because most problems do not go away if blissfully ignored. Rather, this is a reminder to remain positive while being actively engaged in life, mindfully experiencing both the pleasant and the unpleasant.

In the social sciences, two views of optimism have received the most attention—one focuses on *expectations* and the other focuses on *explanations*. When it comes to their expectations, optimists expect good outcomes. When they take a college course, they anticipate they will do well. When they seek a promotion, they are confident they will get the job. This perspective is a source of motivation for optimists, helping them take an active role in seeking the best in life and overcoming the obstacles in their way.[14]

The other perspective on optimism focuses on explanations. From this perspective, a positive view of life is the result of how we explain negative experiences. When dealing with the challenges of life, optimists understand they cannot control everything and recognize that many problems are caused by external factors. They attribute negative events or experiences to causes outside of themselves rather than to stable internal flaws. Optimistic individuals also believe a bad experience is not likely to repeat itself (unlike pessimists, who believe similar bad experiences will continue to occur). Further, optimists believe that a bad outcome in one realm does not mean bad things will happen in other realms. In contrast, pessimists generalize failure in one area of life to all areas of life.[15, 16]

If optimists lose their job, they explain their misfortune in terms of external causes like the overall job market, general downsizing in an industry, or capricious hiring and firing practices. They explain their negative experience as an isolated event and anticipate this kind of problem will not reappear in their next job. Optimists also avoid generalizing; they may be temporarily unemployed, but they believe they will continue to have overall success.

Pause Points

The research cited in the previous section suggests we get the most out of our day when we view ourselves as valuable, capable, and blessed, and when we have a positive, optimistic perspective on life. Let us turn our attention to the Pause Point process with the goal of assimilating these positive perspectives into our lives.

Reflect

In chapter one, I shared that I begin most days by reflecting on the positive interactions I have with others. Let me expand on this, because there is more to this routine. In addition to meditating on relationships, I also consider the positive things I see in myself—my capabilities, value, blessings, and hope.

If you wish to give this a try, find a quiet spot and sit or recline in a comfortable, relaxed position and allow your attention to shift to your breathing. Simply breathe. If you become distracted, just allow your attention to return to your breathing. After a minute or two, focus on all that is positive about you. Rewind your life over the past few days, savoring the good that has occurred. Reflect on your capabilities and accomplishments. They need not be large; in fact, most are so small, they easily pass by without any recognition or fanfare. You may have read a book, walked in the park, or reached out to a friend. Consider what others have offered you and the simple blessings of life. Let your mind reflect on your uniqueness and your value. Focus your attention on the qualities that make you who you are—your smile, touch, humor, spontaneity, intuition, wisdom, humility, intelligence, or potential. Consider what is good in your life right now.

While doing this, savor the positive feelings that naturally arise. Dwell on these feelings, allowing them to elevate your mood. Carry these positive feelings with you and let them energize your day.

Continue this time of introspection and reflection by completing the healthy thinking questionnaire. Based on your habitual thoughts, indicate your level of agreement with each of the statements provided. Once you have completed the questionnaire, summarize your answers by following the instructions for the healthy thinking summary form.

Healthy Thinking Questionnaire

	Strongly Disagree — Strongly Agree
1. I'm a valuable person.	1 2 3 4 5
2. My thoughts and feelings are important.	1 2 3 4 5
3. I can do most things I try.	1 2 3 4 5
4. I'm able to face most challenges.	1 2 3 4 5
5. I have many things for which I'm thankful.	1 2 3 4 5
6. I'm grateful for what others do for me.	1 2 3 4 5
7. I'm satisfied with my current situation.	1 2 3 4 5
8. I have a good life.	1 2 3 4 5

Healthy Thinking Summary Form	Sub-Totals
I'm valuable (add scores from items 1 and 2).	
I'm capable (add scores from items 3 and 4).	
I'm blessed (add scores from items 5 and 6).	

I'm optimistic (add scores from items 7 and 8).	
Total (add scores from items 1-8)	

This questionnaire is designed to help you compare your thought patterns with the healthy thought patterns described earlier in this chapter. A total score close to forty indicates relative health. Your sub-total scores on the individual areas of healthy thinking will range from two to ten. The closer your score is to ten, the healthier your thinking is in that particular area. If your score on the *I'm Valuable* items is a nine, then you believe that you are valuable and have something important to offer. If your score on the *I'm Capable* items is a three, your thinking in this area may not be as healthy as it could be.

Dream

When we pause to consider our habitual thoughts, we may discover we are hard on ourselves. In fact, we might learn we are brutal, if not cruel. If this is the case for you, you are in good company; while it may seem counterintuitive, there are many very successful, highly competent, well-respected individuals who do not think very highly of themselves.

If this is your experience, I hope you are not discouraged. Take solace in the fact that you are not alone. Begin today by imagining a future where your thought life works in synergy with your efforts to live well. You may not be entirely pleased with your current thoughts, but change is possible. The goal, the dream, is to replace unhealthy thoughts with thoughts reminding you that you are valuable, capable, and blessed and that life is good.

Plan

The plan for developing this kind of healthy thinking is a two-step process, which involves *identifying* the thoughts currently populating our minds, and when necessary, *replacing* them. The goal is to replace negative thoughts—the pessimistic ones dragging us down—with positive thoughts that build us up.

It is important to note that both steps of this plan are critical to our success. If we never identify our habitual thoughts, they will continue to have a hidden impact. But just identifying them is not enough. For change to occur, we must replace the negative, pessimistic thoughts with more positive, optimistic ones.

So how can we make healthy thinking a normal part of our day-to-day experience? While the steps for changing our thought patterns are simple to remember (identify and replace), like any other skill, they require practice.

To help with this, let me suggest an exercise based on a journal with two columns. The first column is for describing your current situation; in this column, record any significant event or experience. Then, in the second column, write down healthy thoughts relating to your particular situation. These thoughts reinforce the belief that you are a person of value, capable of making positive changes. They highlight either your satisfaction with your situation or your readiness to make a change. They also express an expectation of a bright future; these thoughts are a reminder that you are valuable, capable, and blessed.

I have supplied an example to help you get started; look it over, and give it a try.

Healthy Thinking Journal

Important events and situations	Healthy thoughts related to your current situation
I lost my job.	I have something to contribute in the right situation. I'll find a job that's right for me. I can update my skills to increase my options.
My semester is done.	What a great day. I'm blessed.
Too many responsibilities at home and at work.	I can learn to set better limits. I can get this under better control. I can say no, and I can ask for help.
A successful project completed at work.	This is satisfying. I worked hard on this project. I did my part well.

Healthy Thinking Journal

Important events and situations	Healthy thoughts related to your current situation

Connect

Earlier in this chapter, I noted that one source of automatic thoughts is our prior experiences; there is little doubt we are influenced by our past. If we grew up in a negative environment where our value and abilities were frequently under attack, it is likely we have challenges when it comes to healthy thinking. If it was common for us to hear negative messages about our worth and ability to succeed, it is likely our internal dialogue is sabotaging our efforts to live well. Conversely, if we grew up consistently hearing positive messages, we are more likely to be optimistic about life and face its challenges with positive expectations.

If you were raised on a steady diet of negative messages, do not be discouraged. Do not give in; fight back by surrounding yourself with others who believe in you. It is much easier to be positive when those around you are positive. Develop relationships with individuals who believe in your value and emphasize your strengths. Internalize their positive message, believe what they are saying, and assimilate their healthy words.

Also, reciprocate by encouraging others. Be specific; notice the capabilities of others and tell them what you see. Affirm their value. Be the one who talks about what is good in your life, and see if it is contagious. Let others know the blessing they are to you. Fill your conversations with positive, uplifting words.

As this becomes part of your life, be mindful and pay attention to its impact on you and those around you. You may see a metamorphosis in your relationships with friends, family, co-workers, and even acquaintances. When your conversations reinforce your value, affirm your capabilities, acknowledge your blessings, and anticipate the best, you are laying the foundation for a life-changing, health-giving social network and a healthy mind.

Experience

One beautiful summer morning I planned to begin my day by attending a lecture. Unfortunately, I hit the snooze button a few too many times. It was now unavoidable—I was going to be late. Immediately, a parade of negative thoughts began marching through my mind: "I can't believe I slept so late," "I let myself down," and "My day is ruined."

As you can imagine, my countenance fell, and my mood soured. I experienced a downward emotional cycle perpetuated by mental negativity.

Fortunately, I caught myself, consciously paused, and intentionally began to rethink the situation. I focused on the value of this newfound margin in my life. Because I could not make the lecture, I now had an extra hour in my day—an unexpected gift. I could use the time to enjoy a leisurely breakfast. Taking a few deep breaths, I gave myself a break and considered the possibility that I needed to sleep more than I needed to hear a lecture and I would have a better day because it began at a slower pace. This reframing of my experience changed the direction of my day. If I had continued the parade of self-critical, negative thinking, I would have continued in a downward spiral. By stopping and redirecting, I initiated a positive, creative cycle.

I wish I could tell you this is always the case for me, but I assure you it is not. I am sharing this experience in order to encourage you to pay attention to your own patterns of thinking (identify) and to make changes when needed (replace). As you gain more experience, healthy thinking will become more natural for you. You will become an expert at catching yourself feeding the negativity monster, and you will instinctively stop to redirect your mind. As you do, you will discover a bit more energy, creativity, and enthusiasm in your day. Nurture these positive thoughts, and grow them into well-worn mental pathways.

Quick Start Routine

Jump-start this pathway to health by regularly exercising your mind. Review the goals you identified earlier in this chapter, and set aside time in your life to pursue them. Whether it is completing a puzzle, learning a foreign language, or reading the paper, keep your mind actively engaged.

You might also wish to make journaling part of your efforts to live well. Simply pause during your day and jot down what is happening in your life; record important events along with your thoughts and feelings. This healthy routine may be just what you need to understand yourself better and add positivity to your day.

Three

Bring Out the Best in Others

It is one of the most beautiful compensations of life that no man can sincerely try to help another without helping himself.
—Ralph Waldo Emerson

The food was quite ordinary, but the conversation was amazing. During lunch, my friend Nick described an inspiring Pause Point in his life. It had started a few years earlier when another friend urged him to help with a mission service project in South America. Nick was reluctant; a mission trip was not at all on his agenda, but because of this friend's persistence, he agreed to go. Once he arrived in country, however, his reluctance quickly transformed into empathy, passion, and resolve.

While digging a building's foundation with a small shovel, he had a moment of crystal-clear awareness. Abject poverty was all around, the need was great, and he wanted to make a difference. This moment of awareness grew into a dream, evolved into a plan, and ultimately, has had a meaningful impact on Nick's life (sound familiar?). Currently, he is financing a college education for some of the local residents, operating a school for children with special needs, and providing land for families to raise vegetables for sale in a local market.

But if you really want to see satisfaction and pleasure in Nick's eyes, ask him to pull out his pictures and share the stories of lives that have been changed. Listen as he tells the story of a child with cerebral palsy who, until attending Nick's school, had never fully extended her arms. Or perhaps he might share with you the story of a college student who is able to study law because of the financial assistance Nick is providing.

What began as a trip to construct a building has ignited a passion for life-long service. As a result of this passion, a small piece of our planet is just a bit better. But do not call Nick a hero; he is simply doing what is natural and healthy. He is bringing out the best in others.

Helping and Well-Being

Until recently, clinical psychology's primary focus has been mental illness and the treatment of patient problems. This focus has paralleled the emphasis in medicine on disease and illness. Over the past few decades, however, there has been a growing interest in emotional health, life satisfaction, and personal growth. One finding that has emerged as a result of this emphasis on the positive aspects of human psychology is that those who serve others often derive benefits from their service.

This was certainly true for a group of college students who participated in a research study conducted by the social scientist Jane Primavera. She gathered data on 239 undergraduates who volunteered to help in a literacy program. The students in this study reported that volunteering was personally satisfying and a valuable learning experience. They gained a feeling of competence and greater self-esteem while increasing their commitment to future service. Primavera notes that her "findings suggest that, in addition to the 'intended' outcome of 'helping' and 'being of service,' volunteers also benefit from a host of 'unintended' consequences as well." Her study participants "describe volunteerism as a source of personal growth and efficacy, as a crucial component of their educational experience, and as a catalyst for greater social awareness and future civic commitment."[1]

This positive association between service and health is present throughout the life span. Nancy Morrow-Howell and her colleagues found evidence connecting volunteerism with a number of health benefits in a group of elderly individuals. Their survey discovered that older adults who are engaged in educational and volunteer activities have increased social interaction and they are more productive. In addition, adults who are serving others experience a greater sense of overall well-being.[2]

In an interesting study, Carolyn Schwarz and Rabbi Meir Sendor trained patients with multiple sclerosis to provide telephone support for other patients. These researchers discovered that the patients who provided the support had positive outcomes with respect to confidence, self-awareness, self-esteem, self-efficacy (see chapter two), life satisfaction, personal growth, and purpose in life. These patients also reported less depression, less fatigue, and fewer physical role limitations.[3]

In the final analysis, what we are finding is individuals who serve others receive health benefits from their service. We are learning that helping helps the helper.

Healthy Helping

A compelling act of service described in the New Testament is Jesus' last teaching moments with his disciples. After the final meal he shared with his closest followers, Jesus got up, wrapped a towel around his waist, poured water into a basin, and washed the feet of his disciples. He then stated they would be blessed if they followed this example.[4] Jesus used this final teaching moment to call his disciples to a life of humble service, which, if lived out, would become a source of

Sustainable service is ...
• Meaningful
• Something offered
• Strategic
• Freely given

69

blessing not only to those who were served but to the disciples themselves.

Borrowing from this ancient example, I suggest that service is a personally meaningful experience in which we freely offer information, skills, support, or resources, with the strategic intent of bringing out the best in others. This definition identifies four key components of the helping process: *meaningful, something offered, strategic,* and *freely given.*

Meaningful

For service to contribute to our health, it must be meaningful. If our efforts to help others are demanded from us or motivated by a sense of guilt, the result is predictably anger, resentment, and rebellion. It is unlikely that compulsory service or service done from rote habit will make a lasting contribution to our well-being.

One of the most popular courses at Harvard University is a course on the topic of happiness taught by Tal Ben-Shahar. In his course, and in a book based on it, he claims true, lasting happiness is associated with experiences characterized by the convergence of meaning and pleasure.[5] If an experience is meaningful but lacking in pleasure, it will eventually lead to treadmill-like drudgery. Similarly, if an experience is only pleasurable without any meaning or value, the luster will ultimately fade and what was initially pleasurable will become stale, losing its ability to make us feel good.

I believe these concepts are applicable to our service. We get the most health benefits from service opportunities that are both meaningful and pleasurable.

Has this been your experience? If you have ever assisted someone else and found the experience both meaningful and pleasurable, did you feel happy? Conversely, if you helped because someone told you to, or maybe you did it reluctantly out of compulsion, how did that feel? Perhaps you have been involved in a service project that was totally lacking in any pleasure or enjoyment; if so, how long did you last as a volunteer?

This is not to imply that everything we do to help others will be easy and convenient. Sometimes there is sacrifice involved—even profound sacrifice. However, if there is always a martyr-like quality to our actions, we will ultimately feel disillusioned and discouraged. For service to be sustainable, it is important to seek meaning and find enjoyment in whatever we choose to do.

Along with happiness, satisfaction is also frequently associated with meaningful service. In his book on satisfaction, the psychiatrist and neurobiologist Gregory Berns proposes that satisfaction is elicited by experiences that are novel and challenging. He writes, "I have found that great, even transcendent, experiences can arise if they are juxtaposed with novelty and challenge" (p. xv).[6]

As a physician, I derive a great deal of satisfaction from providing patient care. Each day brings a myriad of new and interesting challenges. Even the most common medical problem is always packaged a bit differently, depending on the particular patient seeking help. Everybody is unique, presenting a special set of challenges. Based on my experience as a physician, I resonate with Berns' research; I find that facing novel challenges gives me a deep sense of satisfaction.

What would happen if our efforts to assist others would begin with a search for what is meaningful, pleasurable, interesting, and challenging? What if we allowed our service to flow from what we cared about the most? I think the world would be a better place, filled with healthy people looking for ways to extend themselves to others.

I have developed a list of questions to consider before getting involved in a particular area of service. This list is designed to help us focus our time and efforts on what we find most meaningful. If we can answer yes to

Service Checklist
O Is it challenging?
O Is it meaningful?
O Is it pleasurable?
O Is it interesting?

these questions, we will discover ways to help others that are deeply rewarding.

Something Offered

A number of years ago, a rumor began circulating that Michael Jordan was going to play a one-on-one basketball game with Magic Johnson. This possibility was widely discussed on radio and television sports talk shows. On one of these shows, during an interview with an NBA player, the host asked who would win if this match took place. Without hesitation, the player, who was being interviewed, said Michael Jordan would win because he had "too much junk in his trunk."

When it comes to service, what we have to offer, the "junk in our trunk," takes on four different forms—*information*, *skills*, *support*, and *resources*. Each of these ways of helping is beneficial when offered in the right setting at the right time

Information is one way we can help others. Whether it is a mechanic's knowledge of cars, a teacher's knowledge of mathematics, or a lawyer's knowledge of the law, we can benefit from what others know, and others can benefit from what we know.

When it comes to computers, my knowledge is very limited. Therefore, when my computer is acting up, I call my son because he knows exactly what to do. He answers my questions and fixes the problem. He provides a valuable service by sharing with me what he knows.

Something Offered

- Information
- Support
- Skills
- Resources

We also can help others by providing emotional support. We rarely reach a significant milestone without the assistance of others. We need others to listen to us, sit with us, encourage us, or simply share a kind word. Those who serve well are often skilled artisans at emotional support. They know when to listen silently and when to speak empathically. After being in their presence, we know we have an ally.

Along with information and emotional support, almost any skill we possess can be used to benefit others. The skills we offer may be as common as driving a car or as specialized as aerospace engineering. They may be as domestic as baking a cake or as exotic as teaching English in the tropics. For example, when I have a project requiring a skilled carpenter, I turn to my dad. Given adequate resources and enough time, he can build almost anything imaginable.

Another form service takes is the sharing of resources. Some individuals are unable to meet a need because they lack the necessary resources—a student may need money for tuition, a homeowner may need a broadcast spreader, or a neighbor may need a cup of flour. In the right setting, the most appropriate service we have to offer is the sharing of what we have. The resource shared need not be large, but it does need to be strategically placed—the right resource at the right time.

When it comes to helping others, some individuals feel inferior, believing they have nothing of value to offer. But let me assure you this is *never* the case; everyone has something to offer. It does not have to be spectacular, brilliant, or costly. In fact, consider your own experience; are not the simplest, most inexpensive gestures the most meaningful? A hand on our shoulder is often all that is needed to inspire and motivate; a kind word can change our day. We do not have to travel halfway around the world, be a billionaire, or perform surgery in order to serve well—often being available is enough.

Service consists of the information, support, skills, and resources we offer to bring out the best in others. It is the giving of what we have—large or small, significant or subtle—in order to make a difference in the lives of others.

Strategic

Caring about others requires an outward focus. Individuals who serve others well have a keen empathic understanding of those around them. They cannot ignore the homeless man in their community, the local teen who cannot afford a prom dress, or the friend who just lost her sister to cancer.

For service to have the greatest impact it must be properly focused. If we take a shotgun approach, we will have a tendency to overdo it, spreading ourselves too thin. We are most effective when we intentionally identity specific targets for our service.

Physicians are concerned with making the correct diagnosis, because proper treatment depends on it. If a diagnosis is incorrect, the treatment offered will likely be ineffective and possibly harmful. If a bacterial infection is misdiagnosed as a viral infection, the patient will not receive an antibiotic that could limit the infection. If an appendicitis is misdiagnosed as the flu, the patient will not get the required surgical procedure. Proper medical treatment is wholly dependent on a proper diagnosis.

Similarly, your ability to serve well is dependent on your ability to understand the needs of others. I encourage you to pause during your day to take an empathic snapshot of your world; raise your sensitivity and pay attention to the needs of the people who cross your path. You will likely begin seeing countless opportunities to serve. A kind word to the clerk at the grocery store or a helping hand to an overwhelmed colleague may be just what the doctor ordered.

Before proceeding, it is worth noting that serving others requires sensitivity. We can be too intrusive and too intent on helping others without respecting their limits. It is possible to do too much for another person, making him or her overly dependent. It is also possible to be insensitive and offer unwanted help. Identifying and meeting the needs of others need not be intrusive or forced; rather, allow it to be an empathic and compassionate response to the needs that naturally present themselves.

Freely Offered

This next part may be the toughest. When offering assistance, we must not expect others to respond with kindness or even show appreciation. While they may reciprocate, their response does not determine what we do. Service is a choice. We decide when, where, how, and to whom we offer our help; it is our gift.

One pitfall I have noticed is a tendency for some people to push themselves to the point of burnout, living each day on the edge of collapse. They give and give, overextending themselves until they are exhausted. The businesswoman with three kids has her days packed full of work, family, and volunteer activities. She is a soccer mom, a school board member, a room mom, and a volunteer at the local women's shelter.

A common side effect of this approach is resentment. If we are doing too much, it is difficult to make our service a gift. While helping others may require effort and sacrifice, it need not be exhausting. It is hard to maintain our health if we feel empty; if we do not care for ourselves, we cannot effectively care for others. If we overextend ourselves, we will ultimately resent the very ones we are trying to help.

Service is the offering of information, skills, support, and resources with the intent of bringing out the very best in others. What is offered may be quite small and require a minimal effort, or it may require significant sacrifice. It may require no special knowledge, or it may be based on twenty years of experience. It is not the effort or the specialized training that is important; it is the intersection of a freely offered gift with the felt need of another that makes our service a source of life-giving health.

Pause Points

As with building healthy relationships and creating a healthy thought life, we can make service an integral part of our daily experience. In the following paragraphs, we will apply the Pause

Points process with the goal of becoming more intentional about our service.

Reflect

It all begins with the question, "What junk is in your trunk?" What information, skills, support, or resources do you have to offer? When asking yourself this important question, do not be too modest or self-critical. What you offer does not have to be special or unique. It does not have to be expensive or require a huge effort. In fact, the most beneficial and meaningful service is often rather simple.

Take a moment to reflect on what you already do to care for those around you. To stimulate your thinking, I have generated a list of *simple ways to help*. These examples are not revolutionary, brilliant, or expensive, nor do they require a large amount of training or experience. They are simple acts that any of us can do.

Simple Ways to Help	
Listen	Be available
Read	Pray
Mow	Give a ride
Dine with a friend	Forgive
Change the oil	Housesit
Laugh	Do laundry
Walk	Join a service club
Clean house	Volunteer
Visit	Run errands
Advise	Shovel snow
Carry groceries	Offer a kind word
Wash windows	Take a shift

Assemble a purchase	Change a tire
Make a meal	Babysit
Overlook a fault	Be tolerant
Hold the door	Walk a dog
Think before speaking	Defend a friend
Phone a friend	Send an anonymous gift
Leave the last piece of cake	Turn the other cheek
Offer support	Anticipate a need
Do more than you are asked	Offer to help
Send an encouraging e-mail	Trust
Offer your seat on the bus	Support a dream
Lend a hand	Tip generously
Be on time	Connect others
Cooperate	Expect the best
Compliment	Provide respite
Support a cause	Tutor
Say yes	Smile
Stand with someone	Give a hug
Help move	*Listen*

It is not an oversight that this list begins with *listen* and ends with *listen*. Listening is essential to the helping process. It is one of the greatest acts of service anyone can offer. It implies that what is being said is important and the person speaking is valuable. Listening is how we learn about the dreams, aspirations, and needs of others.

These *simple ways to help* require little planning and minimal commitment. They can be offered as a normal part of our day. But they are not trivial and should not be marginalized as unimportant. Though simple, these actions are significant, making up the vast majority of the service that occurs on a daily basis. Small things, like these, often have the greatest impact.

Of course, some service requires specialized knowledge, training, or experience. Mechanics, seamstresses, and computer technicians have something unique to offer because they have taken the time to become skilled in their areas of expertise. The musically talented can soothe and inspire. The mother of three has knowledge and experience she can offer to a young mother who is caring for a newborn baby.

What about you? What unique training, skills, and abilities do you have? What special information and resources do you have to offer?

Take a minute to consider what you are already doing to help those around you. Observe your own behavior, and over the next few days, make a list of the acts of service that are already a natural part of your day.

What I'm Doing to Help
○
○
○
○

Dream

With what you are currently doing in mind, begin to imagine a healthier future. How might you leverage your current skills, abilities, and energy for the betterment of those around you? Or consider developing a new skill, learning some new piece of information, or obtaining an additional resource so you can offer assistance in a new setting. Can you imagine learning something new or gaining a resource simply to give it away?

If you are having difficulty imagining how you might serve, look around. Are there role models you look up to when it comes to their willingness to help?

Begin to make your dreams more specific and concrete by setting some personal goals. As I have noted in earlier chapters, goals are snapshots, picturing a more ideal tomorrow. Use your imagination and project yourself into the future. Dream about how you might better meet the needs of those around you. Your goals might identify specific individuals or groups you would like to help, or they may focus on certain skills, information, or resources you could offer. Your goals may also identify skills you wish to develop, with the intent of using these new skills to help in an area of need.

Goals:

O Volunteer for a local non-profit

O Help feed the hungry in my community

O Assist my elderly neighbor

O Learn how to setup a wireless network

Goals:

O

O

O

O

Plan

The next step in the Pause Point process is making a plan—a checklist of the actions required to reach a particular goal. Below is an example of a plan for the goal *help feed the hungry in my community*. After looking over this example, make a plan for reaching one of your goals.

Plan: Feed the hungry in my community

○ Learn about the local need

○ Donate food items to a local food pantry

○ Volunteer at a homeless shelter

○

Plan:

○

○

○

○

Connect

Nick, who I introduced to you at the beginning of this chapter, could not reach his goal of helping the people of South America without the assistance and support of family and friends; he does not serve alone in a social vacuum. The work there is the result of a coordinated effort involving several dedicated and interested individuals. It is not merely his dream; he is connected with a network of dreamers who share his passion and vision.

As you begin discovering new avenues of service, consider inviting others to join you. When you include others, the experience of service is often taken to a whole new level. Share your ideas, interests, and passions, and listen to what others are doing. Synergy occurs when like-minded people pull in the same direction.

Experience

When I spend time with people who are making a difference, I frequently walk away inspired by their commitment to serve. Recently, I talked with a friend who is dedicated to improving the lives of inner city youth. His investment is improving a small corner of our world.

I encourage you to follow his lead and make service an integral part of your daily life, actively seeking ways to help those around you. Look for opportunities where your assistance is just what is needed and then take the risk of getting involved. Mindfully pursue this essential. The result will be a compelling journey filled with challenge, meaning, and pleasure.

Quick Start Routine

Several times a year, my daughter sets aside time to help with a game night for children with special needs; she would not miss it. On these evenings, a number of special needs children gather for connecting, eating, making crafts, and playing games. The parents of these children get the opportunity to have free childcare for the evening, the children get a chance to sing, eat, and play, and the helpers get the chance to bond with a group of very special children. Who is helped—the children, the parents, the helpers? My daughter would emphatically say, "All of the above!"

What gives you the satisfaction that can only come from helping someone else? It might be as simple as greeting your cubicle mate each morning with a smile and asking him about his day or as complex as traveling ten thousand miles to repair cleft palates for impoverished children. Discover what is most meaningful for you, and set aside time at regular intervals to experience the happiness and satisfaction that comes from helping others.

Four

Eat Mindfully

He who distinguishes the true savor of his
food can never be a glutton.
—Henry David Thoreau

Without warning, he was blindsided—one minute playing a competitive game of racquetball, the next lying facedown and unconscious. As the result of a sudden cardiac arrest, my friend Mark went from vibrant, alive, and active to motionless and on the brink of death. Without the rapid response of key medical personnel, he would have become a statistic—one of the thousands who die each year from heart disease.

Fortunately, Mark survived and is now living a new, refocused life. This brief catastrophic moment has become the catalyst for a series of life-changing Pause Points. He is slowing down, taking stock, and reflecting on what is important. He views each day as a gift from God and lives with a profound appreciation for every breath. Strengthening his relationships, growing spiritually, exercising, and healthy eating are now his priorities.

Before this life-changing event, *diet* was a negative word for Mark. Although he knew his eating habits posed significant health risks, he continued to eat foods loaded with fat and simple sugars.

But he has changed these unhealthy patterns; today he eats more fruits, vegetables, lean meats, and whole grains. As a result, he is slimming down and discovering the health benefits of eating well.

Perhaps you also react to the mere mention of the four-letter word *diet*. It is one of those words in the English language that elicits an immediate negative response, generating, in our mind, images of counting calories, eating sources of fiber that taste like cardboard, and fixing tofu a million different ways (can you already begin to feel the pangs of hunger, the guilt of binges, and the total lack of joy a diet brings?). We all know healthy eating is important; it is a familiar item on our to-do list. Yet, I think most would agree it is difficult to follow through on a commitment to eat well.

Before you react defensively or shut down, let me be clear; this chapter is not about dieting—it is about eating mindfully. It is written to help you discover a pattern of eating that works for you; one that is simple, sustainable, satisfying, scientifically sound, and tailored specifically to your needs. Based on a few fundamental guidelines, it is a prescription for eating directed by your feelings of hunger and fullness and the impact of what you eat on a few important indicators of health. This eating plan is not based on counting calories or carefully measuring portion sizes; rather, it is based on your perceptions, feelings, and experiences.

Eating and Health

In modern America, it is hard to imagine a day could pass without hearing, seeing, or reading the word "diet." It is so deeply embedded in our conversations, newspapers, bookstores, and computer screen pop-up ads that it could be classified as a national obsession. Most of us are either currently on a diet or have just quit one. Because of this overdose of information, and because of our own lapses when it comes to eating the right things, we might be tempted to ignore this chapter or scream in frustration as we skip to the next one.

However, what we eat is foundational to our health and well-being.

In 1999, the World Health Organization sponsored a task force to determine the role of diet in cancers of the colon and rectum (colorectal cancer).[1] This task force concluded that fat intake, alcoholic beverages, obesity, refined sugars, and red meats are associated with an increased risk of these cancers. They also found that certain foods are protective. In particular, dietary fiber, whole grain cereals, poultry, and fish are associated with a reduced risk of colorectal cancer. While many other factors are certainly involved, there is growing scientific evidence supporting a connection between diet and the development of cancer in the lower gastrointestinal tract.

Diet and Colorectal Cancer

- Increased risk: Fat intake, alcoholic beverages, obesity, refined cereal products, sugars, red meats
- Decreased risk: Dietary fiber, physical activity, vegetables, and whole grains

Researchers have also observed an association between diet and heart disease (the leading cause of death in the United States). In a review of the scientific literature on this important health issue, G. Paradis and J. G. Fordor report that weight gain increases the risk for developing heart problems; they also conclude that "taken together, the scientific evidence convincingly supports a causal association between high dietary saturated fat and elevated LDL-cholesterol intakes and increased risk of IHD (ischemic heart disease)" (p. 85G).[2] They recommend a diet low in saturated fat.

Obesity and Health

- High blood pressure
- High cholesterol
- Diabetes
- Heart disease
- Stroke
- Gallstones
- Arthritis
- Sleep apnea
- Colon, breast, endometrial, and gallbladder cancer
- Menstrual irregularity
- Problems with pregnancy
- Overall mortality

The connection between diet and health has been the

focus of research by the National Institute of Health (NIH). In particular, scientists from this high-powered research institute have studied the impact of overeating and obesity on a large number of health-related problems. They view obesity as one of the most significant health issues facing the United States in the twenty-first century. In their research, they have linked weight to a wide array of health concerns, including high blood pressure, diabetes, heart disease, stroke, breast cancer, and gallstones. Moreover, they suggest there are significant health benefits associated with losing excess weight, including reductions in blood pressure, cholesterol, and blood glucose (sugar) levels. The evidence is compelling; being overweight is a significant health risk, and losing unneeded pounds will result in measurable health benefits.[3]

The message from science is clear—both the amount and types of foods we eat affect our well-being.

Healthy Eating

There is certainly no lack of suggestions about what constitutes a healthy diet. Open any magazine geared toward health or peruse the health section of your local bookstore and you will find a myriad of dietary recommendations.

So, how do you choose what is best, especially when there are conflicting ideas? Which voice should you listen to?

When it comes to eating well, two questions require your attention: "What?" and "How much?" The quality and quantity of the food you eat ultimately determines its impact on your health. A healthy diet contains the proteins, carbohydrates, fats, vitamins, and minerals your body requires to function optimally (quality). In addition, a healthy diet minimizes your feelings of hunger, helps you maintain an ideal body weight, and keeps your blood chemistries in a healthy range (quantity). To eat well, you must eat the right amount of the right kinds of foods.

But as you know, this is no small task.

Quality—What?[4]

Let us begin this essential by considering the nutrition piece.

Even in America, where there is an unprecedented availability and abundance of food, it is easy to get too much of the wrong kinds of food and too little of the right kinds. It is also easy to get too much of the right kinds of food.

To get the right foods in our diet (i.e., proper nutrition), it is helpful to pay attention to three fundamental nutrients (macronutrients)—carbohydrates, fats, and proteins. Each of these nutrients perform critical roles in our bodies. We require each of them, but nutritional scientists have demonstrated they are not all equal when it comes to our health. Some carbohydrates and fats are better than their counterparts, and some sources of protein are better than others.

In this section, I offer three guidelines designed to leverage all the benefits of these macronutrients while avoiding some of their pitfalls. These guidelines can help us develop a simple, sustainable, and satisfying plan for healthy eating.

> **Nutrition Guidelines**
>
> - Better Carbohydrates: Eat a variety of fruits, vegetables, and whole grains
> - Better Fats: Eat unsaturated fats as the primary source of fat
> - Better Proteins: Eat plant sources of protein and low-fat animal sources of protein

Guideline #1: Better Carbohydrates—Eat a variety of fruits, vegetables, and whole grains

Carbohydrates are simple sugar molecules linked together in complex chains. When ingested, these complex chains are broken down into their component sugars and absorbed into the blood stream. These sugars (i.e. simple carbohydrates) are a valuable source of energy, powering a myriad of life-sustaining activities. In addition, the indigestible carbohydrates from plants are an important source of dietary fiber. Fiber is known to lower the risk of heart disease, diverticular disease (i.e., inflammation of the colon), and diabetes. Carbohydrates are essential to health, providing both energy and fiber.

But it is important to note that some dietary sources of carbohydrates are better for us than others. Research indicates the key to better, healthier carbohydrates is the speed with which they are digested and absorbed. In general, the slower they are broken down into their component sugars and absorbed into our blood stream, the better they are for us; conversely, the more rapidly they reach the blood stream, the worse they are for us.

If we eat a carbohydrate that is quickly broken down, the sugar it contains causes a rapid increase in our blood sugar level. This increase is followed by the release of insulin and a sharp decline in blood sugar. The impact on us is a sugar rollercoaster. The peak in blood sugar is experienced as an increase in energy and alertness. Then, as our blood sugar level drops, we experience hunger, fatigue, and a strong desire for the next source of rapidly absorbed carbohydrates. In the short-term, large and rapid blood sugar fluctuations prompt us to eat too much; in the long term, they make us more prone to weight gain and diabetes.[5]

What has been your experience when you have eaten carbohydrates from white bread, pastries, a candy bar, or a carbonated drink? Perhaps you have been on a diet that limits fats and encourages carbohydrate consumption, or perhaps you love to eat breads and pastries. Regardless, after consuming a sugar-based meal or snack, do you experience a surge of energy and feelings of euphoria, quickly followed by lethargy, hunger, and a determined search for the next sugar fix?

The solution to this physical and emotional rollercoaster is not eliminating or severely restricting carbohydrate consumption; rather, the solution is eating healthier sources of this important macronutrient. We can limit sugar highs and lows by eating the slowly absorbed carbohydrates found in fruits, vegetables, and whole grains.

Yes, it turns out our mothers were right: fruits and vegetables are good for us. These plant-based foods provide a natural source of slowly absorbed carbohydrates, resulting in a healthier blood sugar profile with less pronounced peaks and troughs. Plus, we get the added benefit of dietary fiber and a whole host of other vitamins and minerals (micronutrients). These foods should be staples in our diet.

When it comes to fruits and vegetables, variety is important. While we might be tempted to exclusively eat our favorites, each of these foods has its own unique profile of valuable vitamins and minerals. By eating a variety of fruits and vegetables, we get the widest possible spectrum of healthy nutrients. Plus, there is another benefit—variety makes meals more interesting and pleasurable. From apples to zucchinis, it is hard to get bored with the countless smells, textures, and tastes offered by these foods.

Raw fruits and vegetables provide the greatest concentration of fiber and nutrients, and they release their sugar content more slowly. However, it seems unrealistic and unduly restrictive to always eat vegetables without cooking them or adding something to enhance taste. I suggest you use personal judgment and moderation. Steam your zucchini rather than frying it. When you eat broccoli, have a small amount of cheese sauce on the side. Also, you might be surprised how much flavor is added by using common spices like garlic, cilantro, black pepper, or cumin. Be creative, experiment, and try different things.

Along with fruits and vegetables, whole grains are good sources of the better, more slowly digested carbohydrates. This guideline is a difficult one for me because I love the refined grains in breads, baked goods, and pasta. Unfortunately, while refined grains satisfy my palate, they are not as healthy as their whole-grain counterparts. The refining process removes fiber and many of the naturally occurring nutrients, leaving only the rapidly digested carbohydrates.

When we eat all parts of a grain—bran, germ, and endosperm (i.e., whole grains), we do not experience abrupt changes in our blood sugar. Moreover, whole grains contain fiber and a variety of other health-promoting nutrients.

The message from science is clear: *eat fruits, vegetables, and whole grains.* These foods provide better, healthier carbohydrates (the ones that are absorbed[6] more slowly), and they provide the fuel, fiber, vitamins, and minerals necessary for a healthy life.

Guideline #2: Better Fats—Eat unsaturated fats as the primary source of fat

Some diets vilify fats, causing us to stand in line at the potato bar or bagel shop with the assumption that carbohydrates are better for us than fats. But when it comes to dietary fat, abstinence is not the answer. Instead, we should choose better fats. Modern research tells us to eat foods containing monounsaturated fats and polyunsaturated fats, while avoiding trans fats and limiting saturated fats.

Sources of Unsaturated Fats

- Monounsaturated Fats: Oils (olive, peanut, and canola), most nuts, and avocados
- Polyunsaturated Fats: Plant oils (corn and soybean), seeds, and fatty fish (salmon and tuna)

Trans fats are generated when hydrogen is added to vegetable oils during a process called *hydrogenation.* Because of their implication in a wide variety of health problems, it is best to eliminate these fats when possible. Trans fats are found in vegetable shortenings, some margarines, crackers, cookies, snack foods, and other foods made with or fried in oils. Fortunately, since their risk has become recognized, many restaurants and food manufacturers are limiting their use (information on trans fats is now available on food labels).

We should also limit saturated fats. These fats are found in meat (especially red meat), dairy products, and a few vegetable oils (palm and coconut oil). We can reduce these fats in our diets by eating lean meats and low-fat dairy products.

In contrast to trans and saturated fats, the monounsaturated fats and polyunsaturated fats found in plant oils, nuts, and fish have a more favorable health profile. Walter Willett, author of *Eat, Drink, and Be Healthy*, writes: "Cutting back on all types of fat and eating extra carbohydrates does little to protect against heart disease and will ultimately harm people. Instead, replacing saturated fats with unsaturated fats is a safe, proven, and delicious way to cut the rates of heart disease." (p. 81).[7]

In a healthy diet, we should get the majority of our fats from foods containing monounsaturated fats (olive oil, nuts, and avocados) and polyunsaturated fats (soybean oil, seeds, and fish).

Guideline #3: Proteins—Eat plant proteins and low-fat animal sources of protein.

Proteins are critical to every structure and function of the human body. They are the essential building blocks of skin, muscle, and bone, and they are intimately involved in breathing, walking, talking, and thinking.

There are two dietary sources of proteins—animals and plants. The animal sources of protein include meat, fish, poultry, eggs, milk, and milk products. Plant sources include grains, beans, and nuts.

One advantage of animal proteins is they are complete proteins. Proteins consist of amino acids linked together in chain-like structures. About half of these amino acids can be made by our bodies, but the other half, called *essential amino acids*, must come from what we eat. If they are not in our diet, our bodies will not function well. Animal proteins are called complete proteins because they contain all of the essential amino acids. Every bite of meat and every sip of milk we take has all of these important protein building blocks. Animal proteins are one-stop shopping when it comes to our amino acid and protein needs.

With animal proteins, however, there is one caution—it is easy to get too much saturated fat. Because these proteins are found in animals and animal products, when we consume them, we are also adding saturated fats to our diet. The solution is choosing lean alternatives and eating smaller portions. By eating low-fat sources like fish, poultry, lean cuts of red meat, low-fat milk, and low-fat milk products, we are able to leverage the maximum health benefit without getting too much saturated fat.

The other source of protein in our diet comes from plants. The grains, legumes, nuts, and seeds we ingest offer all of the nutritional advantages noted earlier in this chapter. They are excellent sources of monounsaturated and polyunsaturated fats, and they contain the carbohydrates, fiber, vitamins, and minerals we need. These plant-based sources of protein offer a unique combination of protein and other valuable nutrients.

Unlike their animal protein counterpart, plant proteins are *incomplete* proteins because they do not contain all of the essential amino acids. Each plant is deficient in a certain set of amino acids. Therefore, if we get all of our proteins from a single plant source, we will not get all of the amino acids our bodies need. However, there is a remedy to this problem. If we combine a legume with a grain, or combine nuts or seeds with legumes or grains, we will obtain all the essential amino acids. Another way to get all of the required amino acids is to combine a plant protein with a small amount of animal protein.

By carefully choosing low-fat sources of animal protein and making sure to get all the essential amino acids from the plants we eat, we will have the fuel and nutrients we need to live well.

Proper nutrition is dependent upon the carbohydrates, fats, and proteins we eat. As we have seen, not all of these crucial macronutrients have the same value when it comes to our health. We ingest better, healthier carbohydrates when we eat a wide variety of fruits, vegetables, and whole grains. The fats that make the greatest contribution to our health are the monounsaturated and polyunsaturated fats found in plant oils, nuts, and fish.

Healthier sources of protein are available in grains, legumes, nuts, and seeds, as well as low-fat meats and low-fat dairy products. Better carbohydrates, better fats, and better sources of protein are foundational to better health.

Quantity—How Much?

In order to eat well, it is important to focus on the *quantity*, as well as the *quality* (i.e., the nutritional value) of the food we eat. Above, we learned what kinds of food are healthy, but now let us turn our attention to the amount of food required to maintain our health and enhance our well-being.

This topic often creates a good bit of angst. Just the thought of restricting what we eat can evoke a number of negative responses.

If this is the case for you, let me assure you the eating plan that follows is not based on counting calories or severe restriction; rather, it allows you to be your own guru, using your perceptions, feelings, and experiences as your guide.

A few months ago, my wife was traveling solo, returning from an out of state trip, when she called to tell me a warning light had just lit up on our van's dashboard. I was not sure what it meant, but since she was forty miles from home and there was not much I could do to help, I suggested she ignore the light and continue heading home. As it turned out, ignoring the warning light was not the best solution to this problem. A few miles later, the van slowed to a crawl and refused to go any farther. Ultimately, it had to be towed and it cost us $3,000 to make it roadworthy again.

When it comes to knowing how much to eat, we have built-in gauges (warning lights) that offer ongoing, real-time feedback regarding what is going on in our bodies. By paying attention to these indicators of health, we can avoid a number of pitfalls and learn to eat well. The gauges I am referring to are *mindfulness, body mass index, blood chemistry*, and *blood pressure*.

Eating Gauges
• Mindfulness
• Body mass index
• Blood chemistry
• Blood pressure

Eating Gauge #1: Mindfulness

Eating is often a barely noticed add-on in an already crowded day. We have lunch meetings, fast-food, TV trays, and breakfast in a can. We channel surf while chewing. With our lunch in one hand, we drive our kids to their next soccer game. Could it be we have forgotten the simple pleasure of breaking bread?

Is this your experience? Is eating, for you, a mindless activity squeezed into a tightly packed schedule?

Imagine your life has been recorded on videotape. Then, in your mind, rewind the tape and reflect on your most recent meal. What do you remember about this particular meal? Do you remember a lot of detail, or is it difficult to remember anything at all? Was it more like a sprint or a leisurely stroll with a trusted friend? After you ate, how did you feel—satisfied, stuffed, guilty, empty, revitalized? Try not to judge yourself; simply remember and reflect.

I am the first to admit most of my meals are anything but memorable. I grew up in a family where eating was a forty-yard dash. Food was inhaled in a matter of minutes. Unfortunately, as I have grown older, not much has changed. Today, as I work on this paragraph, I have to put down my breakfast burrito so I can write. When I eat, I am often thinking about what my day has in store or what is next in my life. I eat while standing or moving from one place to the next.

The remedy for this modern malady is mindfulness. I was first introduced to this concept while studying with Dr. Herbert Benson and his colleagues at Harvard Medical School (see chapter six). If you would like to give mindfulness a try, begin by getting a small piece of your favorite food and finding a quiet, comfortable place to relax. Take two deep breaths, close your eyes, and focus on your breathing. Just breathe. Then slowly place the piece of food in your mouth and allow it to rest on your tongue. Feel its texture. After a moment, begin to slowly chew, taking in the whole experience. Be sure to notice all that is happening. What are the tastes, textures, and even aroma of this bit of food? What are you noticing that you have not noticed before? Spend all the time that is necessary to allow the food to completely dissolve. If you become distracted, simply say, "Oh well," and refocus your attention. After you have savored this experience for a few minutes, open your eyes and reorient yourself to your surroundings.

At its core, mindful eating has three essential components: (1) a slowing of our pace, (2) a focusing of our attention in the moment, and (3) a passive disregard of distracting thoughts.

The next time you eat, consider enhancing the experience by eating mindfully. Choose a location as free from distraction as possible. Create enough margin in your schedule so you can slow down, pause, and fully engage. Enjoy the visual presentation of the food. Savor the aromas. When you are ready, place a small bite in your mouth and experience the rich taste and texture of each morsel. Take pleasure in every sensation. Chew slowly, soaking in all that eating was meant to be. If your mind wanders to other things, disregard the distraction, and refocus on the eating experience. Make it a whole-person journey of discovery, exploring what is unique and observing every nuance.

Is it possible that most diets are a negative experience because we are distracted? Rather than living in the now while we dine, we plan our future. Instead of savoring a succulent bit of food, we are searching the Internet to determine how many calories we are ingesting.

I encourage you to slow your pace, focus, ignore distractions, eat mindfully, and then observe what happens. Could it be that you will naturally find a simple, satisfying, and sustainable pattern of eating? Is it possible you will meet your weight goals, almost by accident, as a byproduct of simple, mindful living? Maybe the word "diet" will lose its negative connotations as you rediscover healthy, mindful eating.

Eating Gauge #2: Body Mass Index

Body mass index (BMI) is one of the most widely studied gauges of overall health. It is a method for estimating health risk based on our weight and height. When this index falls outside a specified range, we are at an increased risk for developing high blood pressure, heart disease, diabetes, and a number of other health problems.[8] There are a variety of ways for us to determine our BMI, including charts,[9] on-line calculators,[10] and simple formulas.

To calculate your BMI, divide your weight in pounds by your height in inches. Then take the resulting number and divide it again by your height in inches. Next, multiply the result by 703. For example, if you are 5 feet 6 inches tall (66 inches) and weigh 162 pounds, begin by dividing 162 (weight in pounds) by 66 (height in inches). This yields the number 2.45. Then, divide 2.45 by your height in inches (66); the result is .037. The final step is to multiply .037 by 703, giving you a BMI of 26 (you may get a slightly different answer depending on how you round).

BMI Formula
BMI=weight (lbs) ÷ height (in) ÷ height (in) × 703

Once you know your BMI, you can use it to determine if your weight is in the healthy range. A BMI ranging from 19 to 24 is considered normal, 25 to 29 is overweight, 30 to 39 is obese, and 40 to 54 is extremely obese. Keep in mind these are only guidelines to gauge your progress toward a pattern of eating that is healthy.

Let me pause here and offer some suggestions for those who have a BMI greater than 24 and a desire to lose some weight. The key is the old adage of the tortoise and the hare: *slow and steady wins the race.* Do not starve yourself;

BMI
• 19-24: Normal
• 25-29: Overweight
• 30-39: Obese
• 40-54 Extremely Obese

rather, eat mindfully. Eat before you get too hungry, and stop before you get too full. Eat better foods, eat smaller quantities, and eat more often. The goal is to lose no more than one half to one pound each week; weight loss that occurs more quickly than this is usually not sustainable. Also, do not weigh yourself more than every few days. Healthy weight loss takes time; it does not help to step on a scale too frequently. One final piece of advice is to increase your activity while you are adjusting your diet (see chapter five). Exercise will work synergistically with your efforts to eat mindfully and lose weight.

Eating Gauge #3: Blood Chemistry

Along with eating mindfully and monitoring BMI, keeping an eye on a few important blood chemistries can help us eat a healthier diet. Over the past several decades, researchers have identified a number of links between entities in our blood stream and a variety of health concerns. Of particular note is the relationship between lipids (fat) and vascular disease (heart disease and stroke), and glucose (sugar) and diabetes.

The lipids that have received the most scrutiny are triglycerides and cholesterol. The triglyceride level, in a healthy adult, is between 10 and 150 mg/dL (milligrams per deciliter). Higher levels of this fat are associated with an increased risk of heart disease.

With respect to cholesterol, the American Heart Association tells us that both low-density lipoproteins (LDL) and high-density lipoproteins (HDL) are important indicators of health. With LDL cholesterol, lower is better—the lower our LDL, the lower our risk of heart attack and stroke. A normal LDL is

Blood Lipids
• LDL: 70-130 mg/dL (lower better)
• HDL: 40-60 mg/dL (higher better)
• Total Cholesterol: <200 mg/dL (lower better)
• Triglycerides: 10-150 mg/dL (lower better)

between 70 and 130 mg/dL, with an increased risk of heart disease associated with values greater than 130 mg/dL. The optimal LDL level is a value less than 100 mg/dL.

In contrast, HDL is a "good" cholesterol; higher levels of HDL are associated with better health. An HDL value less than 40 mg/dL for men and less than 50 mg/dL for women is associated with a higher risk of heart disease. HDL values greater than 60 mg/dL offer some protection against heart disease for both men and women.

When we combine all of the different types of cholesterol, our total value should be less than 200 mg/dL.[11]

Blood glucose is also important because it is an indicator of diabetes. After an overnight fast, a normal blood glucose value is between 70 and 100 mg/dL. If your fasting blood glucose level is between 100 and 126 mg/dL, there is an increased risk you will develop diabetes in the future. Fasting levels greater than 126 mg/dL are associated with active, ongoing diabetes.[12]

Gauge #4: Blood Pressure

Blood pressure is another way for us to gauge how well we are doing when it comes to eating well. If our blood pressure is too high (hypertension), we are at an increased risk for heart disease and stroke. Hypertension is a very common medical problem; the Centers for Disease Control recently reported 32 percent of adults have high blood pressure, and 40.5 million visits to the doctor each year are prompted by blood pressure concerns.[13]

An ideal blood pressure is 120/80. The top number (systole) is the pressure that occurs when the heart is squeezing, and the bottom number (diastole) is the pressure that occurs when the heart is relaxed. A blood pressure of 140/90 or higher is considered to be too high. If you are between 120/80 and 140/90, you are considered to be at risk for developing hypertension in the future. In general, if your top number is greater than 120 or your bottom number is greater than 80, it is time to start paying attention to this important indicator of overall health.

As you begin working with the recommendations in this chapter, I suggest you meet with a physician who can take a medical history, give you a head-to-toe physical exam, measure your blood pressure, and monitor key blood chemistries. In addition, your physician may prescribe medications to help lower your cholesterol, control your blood pressure, and manage your blood sugar. This is a win-win situation; the medications prescribed by your doctor will work in synergy with your efforts to eat well.

Answering the question "how much should I eat?" does not have to be complex or perplexing. To make eating simple, satisfying, and sustainable, learn to pause and eat mindfully. Every time you eat, engage and enjoy, focusing solely on the eating experience. Also, start keeping an eye on your BMI, triglycerides, cholesterol, glucose, and blood pressure. Allow these indicators of health to be your guide.

Pause Point

What follows is often the most challenging and difficult part—transforming theory into practice. When it comes to eating, there is frequently a canyon between our belief and our behavior. We know what to do but have difficulty actually doing it.

If this is your experience, hang in there. Eating well is a lifelong journey, not an instantaneous, life-altering event. Like any journey, there are periods of getting lost, moments of going the wrong way, and seasons of frustration. Yet if you will persist, keep your goals in mind, learn from your mistakes, and celebrate your victories (regardless of how small), you will make progress.

Reflect

If you desire to change your diet, I suggest you begin by writing down what you eat. For the next two to three days, use the *mindful eating record* and make a list of the food you consume. Do not make an effort to change your diet; rather, be a dispassionate scientist and simply record what you eat. Also, record your level of hunger just prior to eating and record your level of fullness just after eating. Rate your hunger on a scale from one to ten, with one representing a complete lack of hunger and ten representing a hunger so strong it is difficult to imagine being any hungrier. Similarly, rate your experience of fullness, using one to represent feeling completely empty and ten to represent feeling completely full. One final thing to observe and record is your level of engagement while eating. Using that same one to ten scale, rate how much you were focused on the eating experience, with one indicating you were so distracted you do not even remember eating and ten indicating you were totally immersed, savoring every bite.

Mindful Eating Record				
Hunger	Time	Food	Fullness	Engaged
5	0700	Whole grain bagel w/ butter & an iced tea	4	3

Over the next few days observe the patterns that emerge as you record your eating experience. Are you eating fruits, vegetables, and whole grains? Are you getting the majority of your fats from unsaturated fats? Are your proteins from low-fat animal and vegetable sources? Are you eating mindfully? Is your eating experience a meaningful part of your day? Simply make these observations. If you are lacking in any of these areas, do not worry—change is possible.

Dream

With your baseline eating pattern in mind, imagine a simple, satisfying, and sustainable diet. Make it your goal to follow the eating guidelines offered in this chapter. Get better carbohydrates, proteins, and fats—the ones that contribute the most to your well-being.

Also, make it your goal to eat mindfully. If you are a multi-tasker, learn to put everything else aside when you pause to eat. Be mindful of your hunger and fullness. Whether you are eating a snack or an evening meal, be fully aware, focusing on the smell, taste, and texture. Take your time and enjoy every aspect of eating well.

Finally, monitor your progress. Keep an eye on your cholesterol, glucose, blood pressure, and BMI. Enlist the help of a physician to partner with you on this part of your journey; he or she can assist you in your efforts to get the most out of what you eat.

Goals:

○ Eat better carbohydrates, fats, and proteins

○ Eat mindfully

○ Monitor BMI, lipids, glucose, and blood pressure

Plan

With your goals in mind, begin planning a personalized, health-promoting diet. Using the guidelines offered above, plan what you intend to eat. Whether it is packing your lunch for the next day, putting a snack in your backpack, or deciding what restaurant to go to, think about it in advance. Engage your mind in the process. Before heading to the grocery store, make a list of the foods you would like to eat and then fill your cart with health.

You might also consider making the *mindful eating record* part of your plan. By regularly completing this record, you can keep track of your progress. If you find you are not consistently eating healthy foods, make a change. If you typically rate your hunger in the six to ten range, you are likely waiting too long between meals or snacks. Or perhaps you discover you are eating when you are not hungry at all (rating your hunger in the one to three range); if that is the case, train yourself to wait a bit before you eat. If you are rating your fullness as a seven to ten before you stop eating, be sure to eat more slowly and put the fork down sooner. Also, plan to eat mindfully. Regardless of how mundane or small a snack may be, stay focused and do not miss any of the experience; make it a ten.

Connect

Having the support of others is an important piece of the puzzle when it comes to eating well. Seek out individuals who share your goal of finding a simple, satisfying, and sustainable eating pattern. Share your setbacks and receive encouragement from those who are walking this journey with you. Learn from each other by sharing recipes and meal plans. It need not be overly structured or time-consuming. Simply begin to share your story with others. Make it a natural part of your interactions so when others join you for a meal at a restaurant, they will expect you to order the broiled fish, eat until appropriately full, get a doggy bag, and bring what is leftover to work the next day. As you prepare meals at home, everyone in your family will become accustomed to having their vegetables steamed. Your ability to eat well is exponentially enhanced when it is the norm of your significant relationships. Eat filet of sole with your soul mates.

You may find it helpful to meet with a nutritionist. Making a connection with one of these eating specialists can be a valuable source of information and encouragement. They can answer questions regarding your particular eating pattern or concerns. They can also give you the individualized help that only comes from an extended dialogue. Your primary care physician or local hospital education department should be able to help you contact a qualified nutritionist.

Because we are social by nature, most things are more pleasurable when we share them with others. Enjoy all of the tangible and emotional benefits of making this Pause Point a team effort.

Experience

Now, live well—live your dream. Mindfully eat a wide variety of healthy foods.

Mark's dietary Pause Point was launched by a near-fatal heart attack, altering his journey forever. You can find motivation in his story. Allow his experience to inspire you to create a healthy pattern of eating; one that works for you.

Quick Start Routine

As you begin eating a healthier diet, I encourage you to set aside time to plan your eating in advance. If you sit down at regular intervals to make meal plans, you will know before you go to bed what you intend to eat the next day. This approach is designed to help reduce impulsive eating and make eating a more pleasurable experience. By planning ahead, you are able to focus on the experience itself rather than being concerned about eating too much or eating the wrong kinds of food. This can make the time spent around the dinner table more enjoyable and less worrisome.

Eat Mindfully

Do not forget the power of connecting with others. To make healthy eating even more pleasurable, you might consider meeting with a few others who share your interest in eating well. Get together with these selected friends on a regular basis to share meal plans, discuss what is working, and encourage each other. Having others involved in your plans may be just what you need to reach your goals.

Five

Exercise Faithfully

Lack of activity destroys the good condition of every human being, while movement and methodical physical exercise save it and preserve it.
—Plato

Tim always assumed he would be a dad one day. He looked forward to all that fatherhood would entail and anticipated the privilege and responsibility of nurturing a new life. When Tim and his wife learned they were expecting, the news triggered a number of unexpected emotions, ranging from quiet joy to anxious trepidation. While he could not wait to hold their baby in his arms, Tim was a bit fearful, wondering if he would do well in this new role.

As he pondered what the future might hold for his growing family, his thoughts shifted to his own health. He wanted to take better care of himself so he would be around for many years to enjoy being a father and perhaps, some day, a grandfather.

This Pause Point experience motivated Tim to start exercising again for the first time since high school. He began by simply jogging for a few minutes; then, he gradually added time and increased the intensity of his workout until he was running thirty-minute intervals on a regular basis. Motivated by a new role in life, Tim initiated a routine that transitioned to a healthy habit. Today, more than twenty years later, he continues to exercise faithfully.

Exercise is the focus of a great deal of attention—countless companies, specializing in everything from athletic shoes to vitamin-infused water, cater to today's sports enthusiast. We are constantly encouraged to increase our level of activity and physical fitness. One web search identified 224 million websites offering instant access to the latest information on this popular topic.

While it might be tempting to think this emphasis on exercise would result in a physically fit population, the data suggest otherwise. Only 65 percent of adolescents engage in the recommended amount of physical activity, and adults are even less active, with only 15 percent engaged in the recommended amount of exercise and 40 percent engaged in no leisure-time activity at all.[1] Thus, in spite of all the advertising and commercial attention, many of us have a long way to go when it comes to getting enough exercise.

How about you? Do you find yourself on the wrong side of these statistics? Are you among the 85 percent who are not getting the recommended amount of exercise? You may be discouraged because you are less active than you would like to be. You dream of a life punctuated by morning jogs, noontime walks, and evenings in the pool. However, you are currently so far from this ideal that success seems improbable, if not impossible. Perhaps you have given up because the ripped bodies you see on television and read about in print represent an ideal way beyond what you could ever hope to achieve.

The word *exercise* is often associated with negative memories of high school physical education class or failed efforts to make it to the gym. It generates images of sweat and pounding the pavement mile after mile. It is no wonder inertia sets in and we settle for a sedentary existence.

My goal for this chapter is to help you transcend this negativity and discover an enjoyable and sustainable pattern of exercise that is tailor-made for you. If you have gotten off track, I encourage you to chart a new course, finding a pattern of exercise that fits seamlessly into your day.

Exercise and Health

Convincing evidence links physical activity to our overall health and well-being. When combined with a healthy diet and weight loss, exercise can help lower blood pressure and reduce the risk of heart disease.[2,3] A study that followed 21,823 male physicians for more than a decade discovered that doctors who exercised were less likely to experience a stroke.[4] Exercise is also one of the keys to managing weight, lowering cholesterol, and controlling blood sugar.

In a review commissioned by the Surgeon General of the United States, the authors report the following health benefits of physical activity:[5]

- Exercise is associated with lower mortality rates.
- Exercise decreases the risk of cardiovascular disease.
- Regular exercise prevents or delays the development of high blood pressure and reduces blood pressure in individuals with high blood pressure.
- Regular exercise is associated with a decreased risk of colon cancer.
- Exercise decreases the risk of developing diabetes.
- Exercise in older adults preserves the ability to maintain independent living and reduces the risk of falling.
- Exercise helps improve mood and relieve symptoms of depression and anxiety.

The scientific data overwhelmingly support the value of exercise. It is a key asset in the portfolio of those who wish to live well.

Healthy Activity

In order to leverage the health benefits inherent in an active lifestyle, it is helpful to consider some key questions, including "How much should we exercise?," "How often should we exercise?," and "What types of exercise should we do?" These questions have been the focus of a great deal of research. Based on this research, the American College of Sports Medicine (ACSM) and the American Heart Association (AHA) have developed recommendations regarding the frequency, intensity, and duration of physical activity in three areas: (1) endurance, (2) strength, and (3) flexibility.[6,7]

Regarding endurance, the current recommendation is thirty minutes of moderately intense aerobic activity performed five days each week. This thirty-minute goal can be achieved in one setting or accumulated by performing episodes of exercise, each lasting ten minutes or more. Aerobic exercise is any continuous and rhythmic activity involving large muscles that results in an increase in heart rate and respiratory rate. Examples of aerobic exercise include swimming, brisk walking, jogging, cross-country skiing, jumping rope, stair climbing, and bicycling. According to the ACSM, a moderately intense physical activity is one in which we work hard enough to increase our heart rate and break a sweat but remain able to carry on a conversation.[8,9]

Exercise Recommendations

- Endurance
  - Frequency: five days/week
  - Duration: thirty minutes
  - Intensity: Moderate
- Strength
  - Frequency: two to three days/week
  - Duration: eight to ten exercises; eight to twelve repetitions
  - Intensity: Substantial muscle fatigue
- Flexibility
  - Frequency: two to three days/week
  - Duration: All major muscle and tendon groups
  - Intensity: Mild discomfort

Along with cardiorespiratory/aerobic fitness (endurance), a comprehensive exercise program will include strength training. By using weights or by exercising against resistance, we increase muscle strength and are able to train for longer periods with less fatigue. The current recommendation of the ACSM and the AHA is to perform eight to ten different exercises, with eight to twelve repetitions of each exercise two or more nonconsecutive days each week.[10] When building strength, the amount of weight or resistance used should result in substantial fatigue of the muscle group being exercised.

The final piece of a complete fitness program is flexibility. The ACSM suggests we develop a stretching routine that promotes flexibility of all the major muscle and tendon groups two to three days each week. On any given day, each stretching exercise is to be repeated three to four times; it is further recommended that each stretch generate mild discomfort.[11]

A balanced exercise program consists of activities which promote endurance, strength, and flexibility. We receive the maximum benefit when these three components are integrated into a consistent routine.

Pause Points

You can use the Pause Points process to create an exercise plan tailored to your particular needs and life situation.[12]

Reflect

To begin this process, you might consider using an exercise log. In this log, note any activity you are currently doing. Record the activity itself, the type of activity (endurance, strength, or flexibility), how long you are spending on the activity, and the overall intensity of your workout. I have provided a sample log as an example. Once you have reviewed the sample, spend the next few days keeping track of your own exercise activities. Do not make an effort to change—simply observe what you are already doing.

Exercise Faithfully

Exercise Log			
Day	Activity/Type	Intensity	Duration
Sun	Jogging/Endurance	Moderate	Thirty minutes
Tues	Jogging/Endurance	Moderate	Thirty minutes
Wed	Weight training/Strength	Mild Fatigue	9 Ex; 9 Rps; 3 Sets
Sat	Weight training/Strength	Mild Fatigue	9 Ex; 9 Rps; 3 Sets
Sat	Basketball/ Endurance	Intense	Sixty minutes

Exercise Log			
Day	Activity/Type	Intensity	Duration

Dream

As you begin to monitor your level of physical activity, you may discover areas you would like to improve. If this is the case for you, take a minute to imagine a more active future. As you have done in earlier chapters, record this future in terms of meaningful and challenging goals. There are many ways to meet the endurance, strength, and flexibility guidelines proposed by the ACSM and the AHA. For instance, the flexibility guideline can be met by attending a yoga class two days per week, the endurance guideline can be met by thirty minutes of jogging five days per week, and the strength guideline can be met by weightlifting three days per week.

After reviewing the sample goals I have provided, formulate some fitness goals of your own.

Goals:

O Run a 10K race

O Join a Pilates class

O Increase overall muscle strength

O

Goals:

O

O

O

O

Plan

With your goals in mind, develop a plan tailored to your unique situation. If you are new to exercising or have not exercised consistently in a while, begin slowly. It may take several weeks or months to reach your goals. This is not a sprint; it is a marathon.

Exercise Plan			
Day	Activity/Type	Intensity	Duration
Sun	Bicycling/Endurance	Moderate	Forty-five minutes
Mon	Jogging/Endurance	Moderate	Thirty minutes
Tues	Pilates/Strength/Flex.	Mild Discom.	Forty-five minutes
Wed	Rowing/Endurance	Moderate	Thirty minutes
Thur	Pilates/Strength/Flex.	Mild Discom.	Forty-five minutes
Fri	Jogging/Endurance	Moderate	Thirty minutes
Sat	Spinning/Endurance	Vigorous	Thirty minutes

Exercise Plan			
Day	Activity/Type	Intensity	Duration

Connect

As you consider ways to increase your endurance, strength, and flexibility, you may wish to include others in your plans. If you are an early-morning person, see if there is a friend who might meet you at the fitness center before work. If you are a runner, join a running club and get the benefit of being around others who share your interest. Walking with co-workers during the lunch hour could be a convenient way for you to add activity to your tightly scheduled day. Find ways to integrate exercise into your family life—run with your daughter, bike with your spouse, or lift weights with your son. You might also consider making healthy activities part of your vacation plans. Travel to a 5K race, ride a bicycle path in a neighboring state, go kayaking, or take a walk on the beach. It need not be too intense or strenuous; simply make it an enjoyable part of your time away.

Many people meet with a personal athletic trainer in order to push their physical limits and accomplish personal goals. These professionals are skilled at assessing fitness level, setting goals, and making exercise plans. A personal trainer can also provide encouragement and support when enthusiasm wanes and good intentions fade.

Be creative—involve others in your exercise plan and then observe what happens. My guess is you will discover greater motivation, leading to an exercise experience that is more enjoyable and easier to sustain.

Experience

Once you have a plan in place, you are ready to take action and experience all the benefits of an active life. As you add new activities to your day, you might wish to monitor your progress by using an exercise log. At the end of each week, compare what you had planned to do with what you are actually doing. This will provide concrete feedback and help you assess how well you are doing.

Quick Start Routine

Jack struggled many years to increase his activity level before he hit upon the right routine; he discovered early mornings worked best for him. He also discovered it helped to have exercise equipment in his home so he did not have to travel to a fitness center. Now, Jack gets up early and makes exercise the first item on his daily to-do list. The results have been remarkable. Today, he is consistently meeting his activity goals.

What will jump-start your efforts to live a more active life? Discover what works for you and turn it into a routine.

Six

Find Peace and Relaxation

Sometime I sits and thinks,
and sometimes I just sits.
—Satchel Page

Consider this twenty-first century allegory:

Stephen, the CEO of a large company, is camping with his wife and two young children on a warm summer evening. After a day of hiking, fishing, gathering firewood, and cooking over an open fire, the family retires to their tent with many fond memories of their day together. Suddenly, Stephen hears a loud crash followed by the sound of a creature pawing its way through the family's cooler. Immediately, he remembers the warning posted at the entrance to their campsite: *"Do Not Feed the Bears."* As his thoughts race, his heart begins to pound, and his mouth becomes instantly dry. He fears the worst as he prepares to protect his family from this very real threat.

Fast-forward a few months; Stephen survived his encounter with the bear but now faces a very different threat, a psychological one—his job is on the line. For two years, his company has not been doing well, and his board of directors is increasingly pressuring him to turn things around. Feeling out of control, he is spending sleepless nights anxiously ruminating about what to do next. His blood pressure is elevated, he is gaining weight, and his diabetes is now harder to control. His mind is always active, trying to find a solution to this difficult situation. He is wired and on edge, yet strangely tired, finding it difficult to concentrate. There is little joy left in his day as he wonders what the future might hold.

These vignettes from Stephen's life describe two very different types of stress. In the first story, the stress is a dramatic physical threat. He and his family were in danger; if the bear were to attack, their lives were literally at risk. The second situation is also stressful, but the stress is psychological rather than physical. While it would certainly be troubling and difficult, Stephen would not lose his life if he lost his job. He is stressed, psychologically, by the total lack of control and unpredictability of his current work environment.

However, if we studied Stephen's physiology, we would discover a striking similarity between his physical response to both threats. The human body has one primary way of responding to stress—regardless of the source. Whether we believe we are in danger of being eaten by a bear or are threatened by the "slings and arrows of outrageous fortune" in the workplace, the body's response is the same. At its core, this universal stress response prepares the body to fight against an attacker or flee a danger. When we are challenged, psychologically or physically, our heart rate increases, sugar stores are released, blood pressure increases, blood flow is diverted to the large muscles of the arms and legs, digestion slows, and the experience of pain is blunted. The body is on alert, mobilizing resources, mounting a resistance to whatever challenge it must face. It is getting ready to do whatever it takes to survive in order to fight another day.

This automatic response is perfectly suited for the kinds of stress we might experience during a chance meeting with a bear, but it is less helpful when it occurs as a response to a long-term psychological stress. It is adaptive when we face an acute crisis, but when prolonged, it initiates a response that can harm our health.

Robert Sapolsky, an expert in the body's response to stress, writes:

> *Stress physiology, as applied to the average vertebrate, is the study of the defenses mobilized by the body in response to physical challenges—being chased by a predator when injured or sprinting after a meal when starving. In contrast, humans have the cognitive sophistication to activate habitually the identical stress response for purely psychological or social reasons—worries about mortgages, relationships, and the thinning of the ozone layer. While activation of the stress response is critical to surviving pursuit by a lion, it is pathogenic when mobilized chronically and many Westernized diseases are caused or worsened by overactive stress responses* (p. 453).[1]

Over the long haul, the chronic psychological stress of modern life can lead to ill health.

Chronic stress is associated with infectious illness, overall decline in the aged, cardiovascular disease, stroke, and sleep disorders. While it would be an exaggeration to claim stress is the primary cause of what ails us, it is certainly a contributing factor that cannot be ignored. It predisposes us to illness and threatens our *joie de vivre*.

Stress—What Is It?

Stress is a complex experience, arising from a dynamic, on-going interaction between individuals and the environment in which they live. It is the natural byproduct of living in a multifaceted, fast-paced world.

Stress is what happens to us (our situation). It is the mental, physical, and social demands we experience. It is the pressure of going to work each day,

Stress
• Our situation
• Our mind
• Our body

attending classes, raising a family, and living in a complex society.

But stress is more than what is happening in our life; it is also our interpretation of what is happening (our mind). Our beliefs, attitudes, personality, perceptions, and thoughts all have a measurable influence on how we experience our world. We even place stress on ourselves by pursuing goals and dreams.

Moreover, stress is a physical experience (our body). When faced with a challenge, our body adapts. Sometimes the physical adaptations are subtle, barely perceptible; we simply feel more alert and energetic. At other times, however, the experience is quite dramatic, resulting in a dry mouth, rapid heart rate, headache, muscle tension, and sleepless nights. This automatic response is our body's way of adapting to a changing physical and psychological environment.

Ultimately, stress is the result of an intricate, on-going interaction between *our situation, our mind,* and *our body.*

Our Situation

To understand stress, we must look outside of ourselves; many of the stresses we experience come from our environment. In fact, everything we come in contact with—both the positive and the negative—is a source of stress.

These stresses range from minor, insignificant occurrences to major, overwhelming events. This morning, as I sit and write, I am bombarded by a number of minute stresses. The sound of my dog snoring causes my eardrums to vibrate, which, in turn, generates electrochemical impulses in the auditory portion of my brain. The breakfast I ate is being digested and absorbed.

As you read these words, what are the minor stresses in your environment? Perhaps it is a slight headache, a cold room, or an irritating background noise.

While background noise and digestion are trivial stresses, other stresses are anything but trivial. Those who have experienced job loss, illness, or divorce know firsthand the negative impact of stress.

The demands and pressures we face have a negative impact on us when they are unwanted or overwhelming. Unwanted stress is, unfortunately, an all-too-frequent companion. Each of us has been touched by strained relationships, troubles at work, and the death of someone we care about. These angst-producing events send troubling ripples through our lives that thwart our best efforts to cope.

Stress is also negative when it is overwhelming. Just when we thought we could not handle another task or complication, we are suddenly faced with a new challenge. For example, you may know a student blitzed by the demands of school, an employee melting down at work, or a mom pulling her hair out trying to keep up with a demanding toddler. It is easy to become immobilized by the many challenges we face, causing us to search the horizon with the hope the cavalry will arrive soon.

Before leaving this section, I want to point out that stress is not always the villain; it has an alter ego. Every pleasurable moment in life—walking down the beach, riding a roller coaster, or kissing a loved one—is a positive stress. These experiences enrich our lives and make a valuable contribution to our health.

Our Mind

We might be tempted to assume our stress level is solely determined by our situation. However, we are not merely passive recipients buffeted by irresistible pressures and demands. Our feelings, actions, and physical response *cannot* be predicted solely from our circumstances. We are active interpreters of our situation, and these interpretations influence our experience.

As humans, we are wired in such a way that psychological and social factors influence how we respond to events in our environment. Research suggests we experience less stress when a situation is under our control, it is predictable, we have an outlet (a means of escape), or it is getting better rather than worse.[2] For example, on the whole, a worker who can limit his exposure to a caustic co-worker will experience less stress than the worker who has no choice over the matter (control). The experienced accountant survives tax season with less angst because she knows what to expect (predictable). The emergency room doctor has a high-stress job, but he has hobbies that provide a means of escape (an outlet). The woman sitting in the dentist's chair copes better with the discomfort when she thinks the worst part is over (getting better). Our interpretation of external events influences how we experience them.

Along similar lines, Richard Lazarus, a frequently referenced stress researcher, highlights the importance of *appraisals* in shaping our experience.[3] He suggests our response to a given situation is influenced by our beliefs (appraisals) about that situation. In particular, we are more stressed if we believe what is happening threatens our well-being. Further, our stress level is increased if we believe we cannot cope with a particular threat. According to Lazarus, when confronted with a difficult situation, we ask two questions: "Is this a threat?" and "Can I cope?" If the answer is yes to the first and no to the second, we become anxious and experience stress.

In addition to appraisals and perceptions, social support influences the level of stress we experience. Individuals who are isolated are more profoundly affected by pressures and daily hassles. In contrast, individuals who have a strong social network are better able to cope with stress. The aging widower does better when he has the support of close friends and family. Similarly, the new student navigates her freshman year with less angst because she has the help of a mentor.

Consider Rick and Debbie, two people in their mid-twenties. Both recently graduated from college with degrees in accounting, and each joined the accounting department of a large firm. Their situations are remarkably similar, but their level of unhealthy stress could not be more different.

Rick feels uneasy about the direction his life is taking. He always wanted to work outdoors in the recreation industry. He was bored with accounting classes, but continued as an accounting major because he was told he could not make money in sports and recreation. Rick is beginning to have serious doubts about his career choice; this new job does not really fit well with his personality or life goals. He is worried he will not fit in and will have difficulty making friends. He did not apply himself in the classroom and is concerned about his ability to succeed as an accountant. As a result, he is having trouble sleeping, has lost his appetite, and dreads going to work.

Debbie's experience is totally different—she loves being an accountant. When she began college, she had trouble choosing a major; but this all changed when she interned at an accounting firm. She enjoyed the internship and returned to college with a newfound zeal for her studies. She is confident in her abilities and has already begun to develop some good friendships. She cannot wait to get to work in the morning because she likes her co-workers, feels well prepared, and thoroughly enjoys the challenge and opportunity. She cannot imagine a better place to be.

Like Rick and Debbie, our beliefs, goals, and support system significantly influence the amount of stress we experience. If we believe we can handle what is coming our way, the negative impact of stress is minimal. In fact, the demands and pressures are viewed as positives—a source of challenge and satisfaction. Conversely, if we feel threatened and overwhelmed, the result is predictably apprehension and anxiety. When it comes to the stresses of life, there is an intimate connection between mind and body, belief and experience.

Pause here for a few minutes to consider the stress in your life. In your mind, review the past few hours or days and identify a particularly negative stressful event or situation in your life. Recall what you were doing, who was involved, and how you were feeling. As you review this memory, consider the following questions:

- Was it under your control?
- Was it predictable (i.e., did you know this event or situation was coming, did you have a sense for how long it was going to last, and did you know how it would turn out)?
- Did you have a means of escape?
- At the time, was it getting better or worse?
- Did it threaten your well-being?
- Did you cope well?
- Did you have the support of others?

As you consider these questions, look for connections between your beliefs and the stress in your life. See if your thoughts shape your experience.

Researchers in the social sciences tell us we are active interpreters of our situation—our beliefs and thoughts influence our response to what is going on around us. If we believe our situation is undesirable or overwhelming, we will experience angst; if we think our goals are unobtainable, we will feel discouragement. As active, interacting participants in life, our perceptions modulate our response to the challenges we face.

Our Body

It has happened to all of us; startled by a loud noise, our whole body stiffens and instantly our heart begins to pound. Our bodies are pre-programmed to react to unexpected changes in our environment (stress). We automatically ready ourselves to fend off a threat or make a hasty retreat. This response to stress has been aptly called the "fight or flight" response.[4] Our body is preparing to resist an attack or flee a dangerous situation.

The Fight or Flight Response

- Increased heart rate
- Dilated pupils
- Increased blood flow to large muscles
- Increased blood pressure
- Cool clammy hands

The fight or flight response is a complex automatic physical reaction in which our pupils dilate, our heart rate and blood pressure increase, and our body mobilizes sugar to meet increased energy demands. There is a decrease in activity of our intestines and bladder, an increase in blood flow to large muscles, a decrease in blood flow to the skin, and a decrease in resistance to air flow in our lungs. We are physically gearing up to run or defend ourselves.

While this response is useful for short-term emergencies, it is not well suited for the long-term, on-going psychological stress we face in the twenty-first century. Most of the stressful situations we encounter last for weeks, months, or years—not seconds or minutes. The demands felt by today's worker are often measured by a calendar rather than a stopwatch. The unwanted vagaries of life, like death, relational strife, and job loss, often affect us for long periods of time. The demands of modern life are more chronic and nagging than acute and urgent; they are psychological rather than physical.

Fight or flight is not an effective response to protracted psychological stress. When stress persists, we begin to wear down, and our health is threatened. Stress has been shown to weaken our immune system, making us more susceptible to infection.[5] It is also associated with chest pain[6] as well as increases in blood pressure and heart rate.[7] In one study, patients who learned to better manage their stress experienced fewer health-related problems, and their health care was less costly.[8]

When faced with complex challenges that last for extended periods of time, our bodies do not always fare so well.

Stress is not a simple, one-dimensional, linear phenomenon; rather, it is a dynamic interaction between what is happening around us, our perceptions about what is happening, and our body's response to it all. It is an intricate dance involving who we are, what we want to become, and the situation in which we find ourselves.

Pause Points

Reflect

Begin this Pause Point by taking an inventory of the stress in your day. Be sure to consider all spheres of life. What is stressing you at work? Are you experiencing difficulties in a significant relationship? Is a physical illness causing significant challenges for you?

As part of this inventory, take the time to look at both sides of the equation—the positive and the negative. Remember, not all stresses are negative; in fact, many stressful events defy categorization. They are a nuanced mix of pluses and minuses. Who would deny having a newborn at home is a life-changing event? But for most, it is a stress that is embraced, because interspersed between crying and dirty diapers are precious moments of deep satisfaction and profound joy. A graduate student may be taking a heavy academic load, but the challenge of mastering the material makes it worthwhile. The physical stress of hiking to the rim of a canyon is well worth the sense of awe inspired by a breathtaking view.

I have compiled a list of common stresses. After perusing this list, reflect on your own experience. Beginning with what has occurred in the past few minutes, rewind your life, identifying the people and situations that have had an impact on you. It could be as minor as being stuck in traffic or as devastating as receiving a diagnosis of cancer. Simply recall the stressful events that are part of your day.

Common Stresses	
A new relationship	Financial worries
A new mortgage	A move
Homework	An empty nest

Vacation	A new diet
Insomnia	Debt
Divorce	Noise
Death of a loved one	A chronic illness
An engagement	Exams
A new job	Deadlines
Traffic	House guests
Boredom	Unemployment
A newborn	Marriage

As you recall these stress-filled moments, monitor your internal response. How do you feel emotionally and physically? As you recall a particularly negative experience, do you notice an increase in heart rate or muscle stiffness? Are you deflated? Are you a little less positive? Or conversely, as you recall a positive event, do you experience joy, happiness, or even love? Did you feel satisfaction from meeting a significant challenge? Was there pleasure in your day because you helped someone else?

Before reading on, take a minute to savor the positive stresses you identified. Pause to reflect on the good that is part of your day. Be grateful, right now, for the healthy experiences currently contributing to your well-being.

Dream

With your current level of stress in mind, imagine a future with a more relaxed, less harried you. Imagine a relaxing journey where you are comfortable in your environment, coping well, and feeling a sense of peace. It is a pleasant place where you are in the process of building protective barriers against detrimental stresses and opening doors to life-enhancing experiences. Dream of a relaxed environment, a relaxed mind, and a relaxed body.

A Relaxed Environment

Imagine a better environment—a place filled with positive experiences that make you a better, healthier person. As you imagine this place, consider what you would have to change in your current life to make it happen. What structures would you need to create? What people would you need to invite in? To what, and to whom, would you have to say no?

Perhaps you have an airtight schedule booked many months in advance. It could be your job is all consuming, leaving no time for family, exercise, or reflective meditation. Maybe you are the volunteer queen, making cookies for your son's first-grade parties, serving at the local homeless shelter, and coaching the junior soccer team. These are all good things, but you are exhausted. If this describes you, consider what a healthier schedule might look like.

Imagine the perfect environment—one that brings out the very best in you.

A Relaxed Mind

Dreaming about a relaxed environment is a good beginning point, but there is more; you must also consider your thoughts.

As you consider the stress in your life, ask yourself these critical questions:

- What can I control?
- What actions can I take?
- What will likely happen next?
- What has worked in the past?
- What physical, social, and spiritual resources are available to me?

When facing stress in your life, focus your thoughts on what you can control, what actions you can take, what has worked for you in the past, and what are the resources available to you.

Positive beliefs lessen the negative impact of stress. If you view yourself as capable and your situation as manageable, you will experience greater peace and approach your day with added confidence.

A Relaxed Body

Herbert Benson has written extensively about relaxation and stress-related illnesses. In his writings, he describes a physical phenomenon called "the relaxation response."[9,10] This response is the antithesis of the fight or flight response. It is a pleasant, relaxed state in which our heart rate slows, our muscles relax, and we experience a sense of tranquility and peace.

A Comparison of the Stress Response and the Relaxation Response	
Stress Response	Relaxation Response
Increased heart rate	Decreased heart rate
Increased blood pressure	Decreased blood pressure
Increased blood flow to large muscles	Decreased blood flow to large muscles
Decreased blood flow to skin	Increased blood flow to skin
Increased breathing rate	Decreased breathing rate
Increased energy use	Decreased energy use

The good news is we can learn to create this state of calm in our minds and bodies. After studying multiple approaches to meditation and relaxation, Benson concluded:

> *The relaxation response can be elicited by a number of techniques that involve mental focusing. The techniques commonly used in the programs of our behavioral medicine clinics include: diaphragmatic breathing, meditation, body scan, mindfulness, repetitive exercise, repetitive prayer, progressive muscle relaxation, yoga stretching, and imagery. All these techniques*

> *have two basic components: the first is the repetition of a word,*
> *sound, phrase, prayer, image, or physical activity; the second*
> *is the passive disregard of everyday thoughts when they occur*
> *during relaxation* (p. 37). [11]

If we find a meditation or relaxation technique that captures our focus and if we ignore distractions, we will elicit within ourselves this healthy physical and psychological experience.

Over the next few minutes, give the relaxation response a try:

> Begin by finding a quiet, comfortable place where you will
> not be interrupted. If you are sitting, place your feet on the
> floor and sit comfortably without slouching. If you are lying
> down, find a restful, relaxed position. Close your eyes and
> focus your entire attention on your breathing. Just breathe.
> Make the movement of air the focus of your attention. As
> you do this, if you have a distracting thought, disregard it
> and return your attention to each quiet and easy breath. Just
> breathe. After you have done this exercise for ten to twenty
> minutes, reorient yourself to your surroundings.

As you dream about a better environment, healthier perceptions, and a more relaxed body, begin setting some personal goals. Add experiences to your day that will enliven and energize you. If you feel harassed by too many demands, eliminate some things and find ways to retreat from the busyness that so easily creeps in. Identify new ways to unwind and relax.

Consider the following example; then make a list of goals that fit you and your particular situation.

Goals:

○ Go on a fishing trip

○ Become proficient at yoga

○ Regularly practice prayer and meditation

○ Delegate some projects at work

Goals:

○

○

○

○

Plan

With your goals in mind, start planning how you might bring much-needed pause to your day. Select one of your goals and develop a checklist describing what needs to be accomplished to reach that goal.

Plan:

○

○

○

○

Connect

When coping with the negative stresses of life, we need each other. Others can assist us at every point in the Pause Point process. We can ask friends how they manage stress. We can ask for another perspective on a problem. We can learn what others do to unwind and rejuvenate.

As we cope with a demanding and challenging world, family, friends, and mentors are often our best allies.

Experience

As you execute your plan, mindfully live each moment. If you spend relaxing time with your family, put everything else aside and be fully present. If you pause in your day to reflect and meditate, savor every peace-filled minute. If you unwind by taking a stroll in the park, be sure to leave your cares at the entrance.

Every waking moment exposes us to a variety of pressures, demands, and stresses. For the majority of us, most of these stresses are positive and make a valuable contribution to our lives. However, when there is too much going on or the stress is unwanted, we can become overwhelmed.

Those who ultimately flourish find ways to transcend these difficult times. They pause to reflect, dream, plan, connect, and then experience a path that protects them from the strains and misfortunes they meet along the way.

Quick Start Routine

To help you get started, set aside a few minutes each day to pause and relax. Below is a relaxation exercise others have found to be helpful.

Find a comfortable chair in a safe, quiet environment. Take two deep, easy breaths. All the way in … All the way out. All the way in … all the way out. Then close your eyes and focus your attention on your breathing. With each quiet and easy breath, you will feel more and more relaxed. Just relax. If you are interrupted by distracting thoughts, simply say, "Oh well," and focus once again on your breathing. As you continue to relax, journey in your mind to a peaceful, serene place. It may be a beach, a meadow, a grove of trees, a picturesque valley, or even a comfortable room—any place where you feel content. Use all your senses to create this image. What would you feel, see, touch, and smell if you were physically there? Now linger and enjoy this imagined place. Spend a few minutes relaxing in this mental sanctuary. Allow your body to relax. Just relax.

After you have enjoyed this experience for a few minutes, reorient yourself to your surroundings, open your eyes, and allow the peace and calm you experience to remain with you for the remainder of the day.

Seven

Connect with the Creator

Stand at the crossroads and look;
ask for the ancient paths,
ask where the good way is, and walk in it,
and you will find rest for your souls.
—Jeremiah 6:16

You cannot help but be impressed when you meet Jerry. He is warm, genuine, and deeply passionate about his Christian faith. In many ways, he has it all together. But recently he confessed it has not always been that way. A dramatic Pause Point occurred that changed everything.

The date was December 24, 1993. Jerry was a twenty-four-year-old alcoholic, spending $400 a week supporting his drinking habit. On that fateful Christmas Eve, he joined a friend at a neighborhood bar. What started as a typical evening of drinking suddenly changed when this friend said he had never seen Jerry sober. Inexplicably, this casual comment inverted Jerry's world, unleashing a torrent of emotions.

Tears flowed relentlessly the remainder of the night. For the first time in his life, he realized the alcohol he consumed was consuming him. He had a serious problem he could no longer ignore or deny; it was ruining his life. To make matters worse, this was his first Christmas Eve away from family. He was alone and in crisis.

That evening, as he had always done as a child, Jerry attended a Christmas Eve service. During the service, he became keenly aware of a huge hole within himself that could not be filled by alcohol. This realization initiated a spiritual quest, which continues to this day. Although both of his parents had a strong faith and he had been part of a church all of his life, he had never developed a personal faith. That night, he vowed to stop drinking and began a spiritual journey of his own.

Today the difference is remarkable. Jerry's intense night of searching, praying, and seeking initiated an ongoing spiritual transformation. While it has not always been linear or easy, Jerry is growing in his faith, mindfully and purposefully seeking a connection with the Creator.

Faith, Health, and Well-Being

Over the past few decades, scholars have begun exploring the role of spirituality in health; and they are making some rather remarkable discoveries. The data they have uncovered affirms what people of faith have believed for centuries: we are spiritual beings, and when we live in harmony with our spiritual nature, we find physical, psychological, social, and spiritual health.

This growing body of research has identified a number of connections between spirituality and health. For instance:

- Religious involvement is associated with less cardiovascular disease.
- For the elderly, the two best predictors of life satisfaction are health and religiousness.
- Religious involvement is associated with lower blood pressure and less hypertension.
- Religious people have healthier lifestyles.

- People who attend religious services regularly have stronger immune systems than their less-religious counterparts.
- Religious involvement is associated with fewer hospitalizations and shorter hospital stays.
- Elderly people with a deep, personal religious faith have a stronger sense of well-being and life satisfaction than their less-religious peers.
- People with strong faith who suffer from physical illness have significantly better health outcomes than less-religious people.
- Religious involvement has been shown to be associated with less depression and anxiety.
- Compared with religiously inactive widows, recently widowed women who worship regularly report more joy in their lives.
- People of faith tend to retain or recover greater happiness after suffering divorce, unemployment, serious illness, or bereavement.
- Religious involvement is associated with more effective coping.
- Spiritual commitment is associated with happiness.
- Religiously active people tend to be physically healthier and to live longer.

When it comes to our health, faith does matter. People of faith live longer, have stronger immune systems, and have a healthier lifestyle. They are happier, more satisfied, and spend less time in the hospital. There is growing evidence that a spiritual foundation makes a qualitative and quantitative contribution to our health and well-being.[1,2,3]

Spirituality

With this connection between faith and well-being as a backdrop, let us consider what healthy spirituality might look like, intentionally limiting our focus to a Christian perspective informed by Christian Scripture, faith, and practice.

If you poll one hundred people on the street and ask them to define Christian spirituality, you will probably get thirty different answers (only thirty because seventy people will ignore you and quickly walk away, hoping you will leave them alone). If you limit your questioning to one hundred individuals from a particular faith group who are, hopefully, too polite to ignore your question, even in this highly select and homogenous group you will get a wide variety of responses.

This wide diversity of opinion occurs because, spirituality, even when limited to a Christian viewpoint, is a complex phenomenon with multiple shades and nuances. To help capture its complexity, in the paragraphs below, I propose that spirituality is a dynamic, living process involving the interaction of four dimensions of the faith journey: *contemplation, connection, expression, and integration.*

Spirituality
• Contemplation
• Connection
• Expression
• Integration

Contemplation

When reading the accounts of Jesus' life, one cannot help but be taken by the flurry of activity—the press of the crowds, dialogue with religious leaders, and teaching moments with his disciples. But in the midst of this demanding pace, we get a glimpse of Jesus' quiet, contemplative life. We read about him praying all night before choosing the apostles[4] or spending time alone after addressing the needs of more than five thousand people.[5]

The example is clear: even in the midst of many demands, or perhaps *because* of many demands, contemplation is a critical dimension of the faith journey.

Those who flourish in their faith have a dynamic personal devotional life; there is a mental, emotional, and intellectual piece to their spiritual journey. They actively seek to comprehend what God is communicating via the written Word and consistently read the Christian Scriptures as their primary source of truth, wisdom, comfort, and encouragement.

In addition, people of faith desire to learn from others who share their passion and beliefs. They read other authors to find inspiration and challenge, seeking insights and nuances of meaning to inform their spiritual walk.

Along with devotional reading, people of faith nurture a reflective life. They pause to ponder the insights gleaned from their reading, reflecting on the nature of God and their connection with him. With wide-eyed wonder, they appreciate the beauty of creation. They also make time to pray, or more accurately, they "pray continually,"[6] integrating this spiritual practice into every aspect of their lives.

The spiritually healthy are comfortable with quiet contemplation. They employ the disciplines of prayer, meditation, and Scripture reading in their efforts to journey nearer to God.

Connection

While solitude is critical to spiritual growth, spirituality also has a social dimension. It is in the context of community that the tenets of belief are communicated, refined, and experienced. As people of faith meet together, they experience the support and challenge that is integral to a growing faith.

According to Genesis, one of the devastating consequences of the fall of Adam and Eve was interpersonal alienation. The account of creation, in Genesis, begins with isolation ("It is not good for the man to be alone"[7]), followed quickly by intimacy, closeness, and connection, then ends tragically with shame, deceit, and death. The connection between God and his creation was disrupted. In a community of faith, this disruption is reversed. In its truest form, Christian fellowship is a redemptive return to the interconnectedness experienced by Adam and Eve before their encounter with the serpent.[8]

In the gospel of Matthew, a Pharisee, an expert in the law, asked Jesus, "What is the greatest commandment?" Jesus responded, "'Love the Lord your God with all your heart and with all your soul and with all your mind.' This is the first and greatest commandment. And the second is like it: 'Love your neighbor as yourself.' All the Law and the Prophets hang on these two commandments."[9] According to these words in Matthew, the Christian's ongoing connection with God and his or her neighbor is an essential element of spiritual health. Those who spend time seeking God in their lives by pursuing his presence are living the greatest commandment. Similarly, the Christian's love for others is a measure of his or her faith.

Faith is deepened when Christians meet together to honor God and encourage each other. I often see this kind of connectedness in the lives of people I know. For example, Mary and her husband Neil's beliefs are strengthened and challenged in a small group that meets in their home. Sam's relationship with God is much deeper and more meaningful because he has lunch with friends who share his convictions. Anna cannot wait for Sunday morning so she can worship with hundreds of fellow believers.

Expression

One of the well-known New Testament analogies for the Church is a body whose parts work together for the "common good."[10] The central implication of this analogy is we need each other to function well and reach our potential. Without the contribution of every person, our planet is a less-healthy place. If we all used our unique skills and abilities, working together to become the people we were designed to be, amazing things could be achieved.

Many of the people I know whose lives have been transformed by the Gospel message are making the world a better place. Sally is helping the developmentally delayed; Jen is dedicated to continually praying for the saints; Larry gives hope to a small group of inner city disenfranchised young men. Each has discovered what he or she was made to do and is doing it. While these people may not make headlines, they are making a difference by quietly, passionately expressing their faith.

Integration

Most of us have multiple commitments tugging us in many different directions. Contemporary life is often complicated, requiring a smart phone and a personal assistant to manage all the changing demands. We Google, call, instant message, tweet, text, blog, and e-mail, hoping to stay ahead of everything clamoring for our attention. The result is a calendar full of daily obligations and a flurry of activity.

Is it possible to make sense of all this busyness? Is there an organizing force behind it all? Does everything in life fit together into an integrated whole?

For some, these questions resolve with a spiritual answer. Their faith integrates the many dimensions of their lives and answers important questions of meaning, purpose, and mission. Their religious beliefs and spiritual practices are at the heart of their personal identity, functioning as a filter for thoughts, feelings, experiences, and behaviors. Spirituality is the organizing thread tying together many divergent aspects of their lives, including their health.

In the preceding chapters, I identify six essentials of health and well-being. While seemingly unrelated, these essentials can all be understood from the perspective of faith. Let us explore how spirituality unites and animates the essentials we have considered thus far.

In chapter one, I suggest engagement, encouragement, caring, communication, excitement, good fences, and synergy are characteristics of healthy relationships. These relational qualities can be understood in the context of faith and community. Christians are called to love one another—in fact, it is one of the distinguishing marks of a disciple.[11] People of faith are to be in significant, meaningful relationships with others—relationships where needs are shared and met, where honest, transparent sharing occurs, and where there is mutual accountability. Healthy relationships and healthy spirituality are inseparable.

Similarly, healthy spirituality is the basis for healthy thinking. In chapter two, I propose that a curious, creative, expanding mind is an important foundation of a healthy life. I also suggest that well-being is experienced by those who believe they are valuable, capable, and blessed.

All of these healthy thought patterns find their source in a God who is intimately involved in the lives of his followers. Christians can be optimistic about their future, because "while we were still sinners, Christ died for us."[12] It is possible to make a difference because, "If God is for us, who can be against us?"[13] Followers of Christ can be creative because they are made in the image of a creator God. And each Christian is valuable because he or she is intimately known by God[14] The Christian source of self-esteem and positive thinking is the unchangeable One who provides the ultimate reason for optimism.

Service, the topic of chapter three, is made more meaningful when offered in the context of faith, because there is an unseen beneficiary when Christians serve. This clandestine benefactor is revealed in Matthew 25:34-40:

Then the king will say to those on his right, 'Come, you who are blessed by my Father: take your inheritance, the kingdom prepared for you since the creation of the world. For I was hungry and you gave me something to eat, I was thirsty and you gave me something to drink, I was a stranger and you invited me in, I needed clothes and you clothed me, I was sick and you looked after me, I was in prison and you came to visit me.' Then the righteous will answer him, 'Lord when did we see you hungry and feed you, or thirsty and give you something to drink? When did we see you a stranger and invite you in, or needing clothes and clothe you? When did we see you sick or in prison and go to visit you?' The King will reply, 'I tell you the truth, whatever you did for one of the least of these brothers of mine, you did for me.'

For the Christian, helping another person is, in a very profound sense, serving the Creator. When people of faith act justly and offer mercy, God is the one being served.

In the chapters on eating and exercise (chapters four and five), I describe the health benefits of eating better carbohydrates, fats, and proteins, and I emphasize the need for an exercise program including endurance, strength, and flexibility. Self-care and engaging in health-promoting behaviors is, from a spiritual perspective, an act of stewardship. When believers engage in behaviors that promote their health, they honor God in their bodies. By eating well and maintaining a healthy exercise program, the Christian cares for the most precious of all gifts, life itself.

The previous chapter (chapter six) focuses on finding peace and relaxation. This essential has an ally in faith. Meditation and prayer have a calming effect on mind and body. When people of faith slow their pace, turn their thoughts toward God, typically their heart rate slows and their muscles relax (the relaxation response). When individuals invite God's presence into their life, they find solace and peace.[15]

In addition, when faced with significant challenges, people who are connected to a community of faith have the resources of that community available to them. They have the very real benefit of emotional and tangible support from others. A community of faith can offer financial resources to those who are in need. Its members can offer help with household chores and childcare. Members of a faith community can provide support through counseling and problem solving, whether formal or informal. When it comes to coping with a difficult challenge, help from others is a true treasure.

For people of faith, spirituality is an organizing, integrating force—it provides a broad interpretive framework for understanding and experiencing relationships, thoughts, service, exercise, eating, relaxation, and more.

Pause Points

By now I trust you are familiar with the change process proposed in this book; you are well practiced in pausing to reflect, dream, plan, connect, and experience. This process is as applicable to faith as it is to the other essentials of health and well-being.

Reflect

Begin your time of personal reflection by considering the questions posed below in the spirituality questionnaire. Do not spend a great deal of time with any particular question; simply record your first impression.

Spirituality Questionnaire	
1. I frequently spend time alone in prayer and meditation.	Strongly Disagree Strongly Agree 1 2 3 4 5
2. I know the Scriptures well.	Strongly Disagree Strongly Agree 1 2 3 4 5
3. I'm closely connected with others who share my faith.	Strongly Disagree Strongly Agree 1 2 3 4 5
4. I'm connected to a larger community of faith.	Strongly Disagree Strongly Agree 1 2 3 4 5

	Strongly Disagree / Strongly Agree
5. I'm working to make the world a better place.	1 2 3 4 5
6. I'm serving others in my community.	1 2 3 4 5
7. My faith influences the way I think.	1 2 3 4 5
8. My faith influences my daily decisions.	1 2 3 4 5

Spirituality Summary Form	Sub-Totals
Contemplation (add scores from items 1 and 2).	
Connection (add scores from items 3 and 4).	
Expression (add scores from items 5 and 6).	
Integration (add scores from items 7 and 8).	
Total (add scores from items 1-8)	

Your total score on this questionnaire will fall between eight and forty, with forty representing a strength on your part when it comes to spirituality. Your scores on the individual dimensions will range from two to ten with two representing a relative weakness and ten representing a relative strength. For example, if your score on the contemplation dimension is a three, this is an area where you might choose to do some work. Conversely, if your score on expression is a ten, this signifies an area in which you excel.

Take a minute to narrow your focus by reflecting on your particular faith journey. In your imagination, rewind your life, recalling specific spiritual experiences. Beginning with what happened as recently as a few minutes ago, mentally identify episodes of contemplation, connection, expression, and integration. Focus on what you were doing, where you were, who you were with, and how you felt. Perhaps you will recall the calm and peace that comes from meditative prayer or the satisfaction you felt when helping your neighbor. Maybe you will experience a sense of gratitude for God's presence in your life.

As you recall these positive spiritual experiences, observe the impact on your energy and emotions.

Dream

When we take the time to reflect on our lives, we often discover areas needing some work. If this is your experience, begin to formulate goals to address some of the deficits you have identified.

At this point, goal setting is likely second nature for you. Remember, goals represent meaningful endpoints you desire to reach. Below, I have listed some sample goals. Once you have perused this list, take a minute and record some goals of your own.

Goals:

O Deepen my personal devotional life

O Help the homeless in my community

O Take a short-term mission trip

O Connect with a local faith community

Goals:

- O
- O
- O
- O

Plan

Now select one of your goals and develop a plan. Be sure to make it specific and measurable so you can evaluate your progress. Do not worry about making it perfect! It may take several tries to develop one that works well for you.

Plan:

- O
- O
- O
- O

Connect

Flourishing spirituality requires community. While your faith has a personal, contemplative side, it is important to have others join you on this part of your journey. As you dream and plan for a deeper spiritual walk, look around for those who might join you. Look for a spiritual guide—a co-conspirator against a secular life. Connect with others who share your dreams of a deeper faith.

Reflect together, express your faith together, and learn from each other as you strive to make spirituality an integrating force.

Experience

Now, live your dream!

With your destination clearly defined, begin to mindfully live out your beliefs. Do not miss the faith-filled moments populating your day. Bend your knee to the Creator; reflect on the beauty of the world; meditate on the Word. Begin to express your faith in new and exciting ways.

Quick Start Routine

People of faith integrate spiritual practices into their daily routine. They take time on a regular basis to read, meditate, and pray. They are closely connected to a local faith community, worshiping and serving alongside fellow believers. They are involved in their communities, making a difference in the lives of others. In fact, people of faith view all of life through the eyes of faith.

Read below how a close friend describes his daily spiritual routine:

> *My spiritual rhythm in listening for God's voice involves my entire day. I have tried to train myself to be attentive to him through Scripture, small talk, hallway conversations, circumstances, other reading, and my home life. As for a specific, intentional practice, each day I participate in a holy exercise. Typically this occurs in the morning, after I run with my daughter. I begin in prayer, sometimes singing. I read a Scripture passage. Normally, it is my practice to read through the Bible once or twice a year. During that reading, I am listening and looking for what God might be impressing upon my soul. Often, I will sit quietly and listen after I have read to see if God wants to emphasize anything. I journal about anything he brings to my attention, often writing a brief prayer. I then read a piece of something*

else I am working through, sometimes a devotional classic. I do my "holy exercise" seven days a week and particularly enjoy it when I have more time in my day to listen and reflect.

Pause at this point to review the goals you identified above, and then settle on a routine to jumpstart your efforts. Mindfully seek a meaningful faith and discover the health inherent in this less-traveled road.

STAYING ON TRACK

Conclusion

Staying on Track

This is not the end.
It is not even the beginning of the end.
But it is, perhaps, the end of the beginning.
—Sir Winston Churchill

A consistent theme throughout this book is that health is more than a lack of illness—it is a journey involving every dimension of life. Those who wish to flourish, getting the most out of each day, engage in the moment while simultaneously seeking a better future. While these individuals are not perfect in their health practices, they are unswerving in their commitment to live well.

Strategies for Success
• Stay in the game
• Create upward spirals
• Mindfully celebrate

This journey, though enlivening, is not a straightforward, linear process in which we flawlessly move from one success to the next. Inevitably, barriers arise, making it difficult to reach our destination.

But do not grow weary and give up! Thriving in a fast-paced, ever-changing world is not just a fantasy—it is attainable.

In the paragraphs that follow, I identify three strategies designed to encourage us when we are confronted with obstacles that threaten our resolve.

Stay in the Game

A number of years ago, psychologist Martin Seligman formulated a theory of depression he called "learned helplessness." In essence, this theory asserts that depression is the result of a perceived absence of control over what happens in our lives. He proposed that if we believe our problem solving efforts are ineffectual, we will feel helpless and ultimately give up.[1]

Seligman developed this view of depression from observations he made while performing experiments with dogs. When exposed to an electrical shock and given no means of escape, dogs in his experiments would eventually stop trying to free themselves. Moreover, after learning their efforts were futile in one experiment, these dogs made no effort to get away even when shocked in experiments in which they could escape. These unfortunate dogs would lie down and passively accept whatever came their way.

It is easy to become fatalistic and develop a sense of despair when it comes to our health. Despite making several starts down the road to a healthier lifestyle, we are often discouraged because we find ourselves on a detour. We continue to feel the shock of unhealthy living, but we are immobilized by our feelings of helplessness. There may be a way of escape, but we no longer make an effort because we expect our efforts to be futile.

You will experience setbacks; but I hope you will not give up. While living mindfully and purposely is not always easy, hang in there—the reward is well worth the effort. If you have tried and failed ten times, pick yourself back up and make the eleventh attempt. Keep trying until you reach your goals.

Well-being is the reward of those who stay in the game.

Create Upward Spirals

We form habits when we engage in a particular activity with such regularity that it becomes automatic, occurring without thought or planning. Our days are filled with countless habitual behaviors. We wake up at the same time, do the same thing at work, take the same path home, sit in the same chair, watch the same television shows, and get ready for bed the same way.

Once established, a habit is difficult to change. Forming a new habit requires determination and practice. We must engage our minds, resist the tendency to fall back into old patterns, and persist in making the new pattern part of who we are. If we will regularly practice, what was once new and awkward will ultimately become part of our routine, fitting comfortably into our day.

This book's fundamental intention is to help you create habits that will initiate a positive upward spiral leading to a better, healthier life. As you complete one leg of this journey, new vistas will suddenly come into view. The young man who discovers the joy of greater intimacy with his spouse begins to seek additional ways to improve their relationship. The woman who travels to Kenya to serve on a medical mission cannot wait to go back. The reformed coach potato is getting so much from his nightly walks he dreams of running a 5K race. There is a deepening, almost irresistible momentum that occurs as one Pause Point experience leads naturally to the next.

I hope you will continue building on what you have learned from this book. Let each new healthy habit be the stimulus for new insights, dreams, and plans.

Mindfully Celebrate

I have met many people who are results-oriented. When they travel, they are anxious to get there. When they start a project at work, they focus on the end product. They are so intent on reaching their destination they fail to take in the scenery or smell the proverbial rose. The downside of this approach is that it is easy to miss the joy of the journey itself.

Let me encourage you to live mindfully, fully engaged in the moment. Nothing is too small to enjoy and celebrate. Appreciate the simple pleasure of an impromptu conversation with a trusted friend. Reflect on the satisfaction inherent in helping your neighbor. Pause, even now, to be grateful for all that is good in your life.

I hope *Pause Points* has initiated an incredible journey of mind, body, and spirit—a journey in which you love the ones you're with, fill your mind with the best, bring out the best in others, eat mindfully, exercise faithfully, find peace and relaxation, and connect with the Creator.

Live a rich, contemplative, healthy life filled with the joy and satisfaction that comes from living mindfully and purposefully.

About the Author

Dr. Gene Harker's professional and personal life is dedicated to promoting health and well-being. He has four graduate degrees (MEd, MA, PhD, and MD) in four disciplines (education, theology, psychology, and medicine) with stints at three Big Ten Universities, a seminary, and an Ivy League school. He has more than 25 years of professional experience as a physician, psychologist, and professor. Dr. Harker is a frequent seminar speaker and is published in refereed journals. He is currently on the medical faculty of a large university in the Midwest.

He and his wife, Lynette, have been married for 28 years. They have two adult children, Alex and Hayleigh. Alex is in graduate school studying Communication and Hayleigh is in college studying Communication Disorders.

References and Notes

Getting Started

[1] Baumeister, R. F., Bratslavsky, E., Finkenauer, C. & Vohs, K. D. (2001). Bad is Stronger than Good. *Review of General Psychology, 5* (4), 323–70.

[2] Lewis, J. M. (1998). For Better or Worse: Interpersonal Relationships and Individual Outcome. *American Journal of Psychiatry, 155* (5), 582–89.

[3] http://www.goodreads.com/author/quotes/32106.Fred_Rogers.

[4] http://www.cdc.gov/nccdphp/sgr/contents.htm

[5] Koenig, H. G. (1999). *The Healing Power of Faith: Science Explores Medicine's Last Great Frontier.* New York: Simon & Schuster.

[6] Fredrickson, B. L. (2009). *Positivity: Groudbreaking Research Reveals How to Embrace the Hidden Strength of Positive Emotions, Overcome Negativity, and Thrive.* New York: Crown Publishers.

[7] King, L. A. (2001). The Health Benefits of Writing About Life Goals. *Personality and Social Psychology Bulletin, 27* (7), 798–807.

[8] Langston, C. A. (1994). Captializing On and Coping With Daily-Life Events: Expressive Responses to Positive Events. *Journal of Personality and Social Psychology, 67* (6), 1112–25.

[9] Loehr, J., & Schwartz, T. (2003). *The Power of Full Engagement: Managing Energy, Not Time, is the Key to High Performance and Personal Renewal.* New York: Free Press Paperbacks.

Seven Essentials of Health and Well-Being

One: Love the Ones You're With

[1] Rozanski, A., Blumenthal, J., & Kaplan, J. (1999). Impact of Psychological Factors on the Pathogenesis of Cardiovascular Disease and Implications for Therapy. *Circulation, 99* (16), 2192–217.

[2] Welin, C., Lappas, G., & Wilhelmsen, L. (2000). Independent Importance of Psychosocial Factors for Prognosis After Myocardial Infarction. *Journal of Internal Medicine, 247* (6), 629–39.

[3] Kiecolt-Glasser, J. K. (1999). Stress, Personal Relationships, and Immune Function: Health Implications. *Brain, Behavior, and Immunity, 13* (1), 61–72.

[4] Kawachi, I., & Berkman, L. F. (2001). Social Ties and Mental Health. *Journal of Urban Health: Bulletin of the New York Academy of Medicine, 78* (3), 458–67.

[5] Loehr, J., & Schwartz, T. (2003). *The Power of Full Engagement: Managing Energy, Not Time, is the Key to High Performance and Personal Renewal.* New York: Free Press.

[6] Gottman, J. M. (1994). *What Predicts Divorce?: The Relationship Between Marital Processes and Marital Outcomes.* Hillsdale, NJ: Lawrence Erlbaum Associates.

[7] Peck, M. S. (1978). *The Road Less Traveled: A New Psychology of Love, Traditional Values and Spiritual Growth*. New York: Simon and Schuster.

[8] Gable, S. L., Reis, H. T., Impett, E. A., & Asher, A. E. (2004). What Do You Do When Things Go Right? The Intrapersonal and Interpersonal Benefits of Sharing Positive Events. *Journal of Personality and Social Psychology, 87* (2), 228–45.

[9] King, L. A. (2001). The Health Benefits of Writing About Life Goals. *Personality and Social Psychology Bulletin, 27* (7), 798–807.

Two: Fill Your Mind With The Best

[1] Peterson, C., & Bossio, L. M. (2001). Optimism and Physical Well-Being. In E. C. Chang (Ed.), *Optimism & Pessimism: Implications for Theory, Research, and Practice* (pp.127–46). Washington DC: American Psychological Association.

[2] Brannon, L., & Feist, J. (2009). *Health Psychology: An Introduction to Behavior and Health.* (7th Ed.) Belmont, CA: Wadsworth.

[3] Small, G. (2002). *The Memory Bible: An Innovative Strategy For Keeping Your Brain Young.* New York: Hyperion.

[4] Some readers of this book will suffer with depression, a serious illness that can have a profound impact. This book is not designed to treat depression or any other illness or problem. If you are depressed, please seek care from a trained professional—a primary care physician, psychiatrist, psychologist, social worker, or counselor.

[5] Hurst, D. F., Boswell, D. L., Boogaard, S. E., & Watson, M. W. (1997). The Relationship of Self-Esteem to the Health-Related Behaviors of the Patients of a Primary Care Clinic. *Archives of Family Medicine, 6* (1), 67–70.

[6] Cheng, H., & Furnham, A. (2003). Personality, Self-Esteem, and Demographic Predictions of Happiness and Depression. *Personality and Individual Differences, 34* (6), 921–42.

[7] Bandura, A. (1977). Self-Efficacy: Toward a Unifying Theory of Behavior Change. *Psychology Review, 84,* 191–215.

[8] Strecher, V. J., DeVellis, B. M., Becker, M. H., & Rosenstock, I. M. (1986). The Role of Self-Efficacy in Achieving Health Behavior Change. *Health Education Quarterly, 13* (1), 73–91.

[9] Brekke, M., Hjortdahl, P., & Kvien, T. K. (2001). Self-Efficacy and Health Status in Rheumatoid Arthritis: A Two-Year Longitudinal Observational Study. *Rheumatology, 40,* 387–92.

[10] Jackson, E. S., Tucker C. M., & Herman, K. C. (2007). Health Value, Perceived Social Support and Health Self-Efficacy as Factors in a Health-Promoting Lifestyle. *Journal of American College of Health, 56* (1), 69–74.

[11] Maddux, J. E. (2005). Self-Efficacy: The Power of Believing You Can. In C. R. Snyder & S. J. Lopez (Eds.), *Handbook of Positive Psychology* (pp. 277–87). Oxford, UK: Oxford University Press.

[12] Emmons, R. A., & McCullough, M. E. (2003). Counting Blessings Versus Burdens: An Experimental Investigation of Gratitude and Subjective Well-Being in Daily Life. *Journal of Personality and Social Psychology, 84* (2), 377–89.

[13] Lyubomirsky, S. (2007). *The How of Happiness: A Scientific Approach to Getting the Life You Want.* New York: The Penguin Press.

[14] Carver, C. S., Scheier, M. F., Miller, C., & Fulford, D. (2009.) Optimism. In C. R. Snyder & S. J. Lopez (Eds.), *Oxford Handbook of Positive Psychology,* (pp. 303–12). Oxford, UK: Oxford University Press.

[15] Peterson, C., & Steen, T. A. (2009). Optimistic Explanatory Style. In C. R. Snyder & S. J. Lopez (Eds.), *Oxford Handbook of Positive Psychology* (pp. 313–22). Oxford, UK: Oxford University Press.

[16] Snyder, C. R., & Lopez, S. J. (2007). *Positive Psychology: The Science and Practical Explorations of Human Strength.* Thousand Oaks, CA: Sage Publications.

Three: Bring Out the Best in Others

[1] Primavera, J. (1999). The Unintended Consequences of Volunteerism: Positive Outcomes for Those Who Serve. *Journal of Prevention & Intervention in the Community, 18* (1 & 2), 125–40.

[2] Morrow-Howell, N., Kinnevy, S., & Mann, M. (1999). The Perceived Benefits of Participating in Volunteer and Educational Activities. *Journal of Gerontolgical Social Work, 32* (2), 65–80.

[3] Schwartz, C. E., & Sendor, M. (1999). Helping Others Helps Oneself: Response Shift Effects in Peer Support. *Social Science & Medicine, 48*, 1563–75.

[4] John 13:14–17.

[5] Ben-Shahar, T. (2007). *Happier: Learn The Secrets of Daily Joy and Lasting Fulfillment.* New York: McGraw Hill.

[6] Berns, G. (2005). *Satisfaction: The Science of Finding True Fulfillment.* New York: Henry Holt and Company.

Four: Eating Mindfully

[1] Scheppach, W., Bingham, S., Boutron-Ruault, M.C., et al. (1999). WHO Consensus Statement on the Role of Nutrition

in Colorectal Cancer. *European Journal of Cancer Prevention,* 8, 57–62.

[2] Paradis, G., & Fodor, J. G. (1999). Diet and the Prevention of Cardiovascular Diseases. *Canadian Journal of Cardiology,* 15 (Supplement G), 81G–88G.

[3] http://www.nhlbi.nih.gov/guidelines/obesity/ob_home.htm

[4] Please note these recommendations are for healthy adults; newborn babies, infants, children, and adolescents have different nutritional requirements. Women who are in the childbearing years, pregnant, or lactating do not have the same nutritional needs as other adults. Also, individuals with chronic illness or individuals healing from surgery need additional nutritional support. If you have special needs, please consult your physician.

[5] Agatston, A. (2003). *The South Beach Diet: The Delicious, Doctor-Designed, Foolproof Plan for Fast Healthy Weight Loss.* New York: St. Martin's Press.

[6] Individual fruits and vegetables vary greatly with respect to how rapidly their carbohydrates are absorbed. For example, the carbohydrates in a watermelon affect blood sugar differently than the carbohydrates found in an apple; the rise in blood sugar caused by raw carrots is different than the rise in blood sugar caused by boiled peas.

Researchers are testing carbohydrate-rich foods with the goal of observing how rapidly blood sugar rises after they are eaten. Each food tested is assigned a number between zero and one hundred; this number is called the *Glycemic Index* (GI). The closer a particular food's GI is to one hundred, the more rapidly its carbohydrates are absorbed; the closer a food's GI is to zero, the more slowly its carbohydrates are absorbed. Based on this research, the GI for watermelon is seventy-two, an apple is forty, and raw carrots are sixteen. As you can see from these numbers, the carbohydrates from an apple are more slowly absorbed than the carbohydrates from a watermelon, and raw carrots are very stingy when it comes giving up their sugars. For a web-based list of GIs for particular foods, see www.glycemicindex.com.

[7] Willett, W. C. (2005). *Eat, Drink, and Be Healthy: The Harvard Medical School Guide To Healthy Eating.* New York: Simon & Schuster.

[8] Fat distribution is an important predictor of health problems. Individuals who carry their extra weight over their abdomen are at an increased risk for developing a variety of illnesses. In particular, the risk of associated medical problems is higher in men who have a waist circumference greater than forty inches and higher in women who have a waist circumference greater than thirty-five inches.

[9] http://www.nhlbi.nih.gov/guidelines/obesity/bmi_tbl.pdf.

[10] www.nhlbisupport.com/bmi/.

[11] http://www.americanheart.org/presenter.jhtml?identifier=183# total.

[12] All of the recommendations in this section are based on information gathered from a large number of individuals. The optimal lipid profile and glucose level for you, as an individual, may vary from these guidelines. Please discuss what is best for you with your physician.

[13] http://www.cdc.gov/nchs/fastats/hyprtens.htm.

Five: Exercise Faithfully

[1] http://www.healthypeople.gov.

[2] PREMIER Collaborative Research Group (2003). Effects of Comprehensive Lifestyle Modification on Blood Pressure

Control. *The Journal of the American Medical Association, 289* (16), 2083–93.

[3] Goede, P., Vedel, P., Larsen, N., Jensen, G. V., Parving, H. H., & Pedersen, O. (2003). Multifactorial Intervention and Cardiovascular Disease in Patients with Type 2 Diabetes. *The New England Journal of Medicine, 348* (5), 383–93.

[4] Lee, I. M., Hennekens, C. H., Berger, K., Buring, J. E., & Manson, J. E. (1999). Exercise and Risk of Stroke in Male Physicians. *Stroke, 30*, 1–6.

[5] http://www.cdc.gov/nccdphp/sgr/contents.htm.

[6] Haskell, W. L., Lee, I. M., Pate, R. R., Powell, K. E., Blair, S. N., Franklin, B. A., et al. (2007). Physical Activity and Public Health: Updated Recommendations for Adults from the American College of Sports Medicine and the American Heart Association. *Circulation, 116*, 1081–93.

[7] Pollock, M. L., Gaesser, G. A., Butcher, J. D., Després, J. P., Dishman, R. K., Franklin, B. A., & Garber, C. E. (1998). ACSM Position Stand: The Recommended Quantity and Quality of Exercise for Developing and Maintaining Cardiorespiratory and Muscular Fitness, and Flexibility in Healthy Adults. *Medicine & Science in Sports & Exercise, 30* (6), 975–91.

[8] Another option for meeting the endurance recommendations from the American Heart Association and the American College of Sports Medicine is vigorous aerobic physical activity for a minimum of twenty minutes, three times a week. A vigorous activity is one that causes rapid breathing and a substantial increase in heart rate.

[9] The endurance recommendations in chapter five are minimum requirements designed to help maintain health and reduce the risk of chronic disease in healthy adults between the ages of eighteen and sixty-five. Some evidence suggests additional

health benefits may be gained by getting even more exercise. For example, to help "manage body weight and prevent gradual, unhealthy weight gain in adulthood" it is suggested we get sixty minutes of moderate to vigorous activity on most days of the week while watching caloric intake (see chapter four). Further, to maintain weight loss, we may need to engage in sixty to ninety minutes of daily moderate-intensity activity (http://www.health.gov/dietaryguidelines/dga2005/document/html/chapter4.htm).

[10] When beginning a strengthening program for the first time, it is often beneficial to solicit the help of an athletic trainer. An experienced trainer can help select an appropriate set of exercises and demonstrate proper technique.

[11] American College of Sports Medicine. (2009). *ACSM's Guidelines for Exercise Testing and Prescription* (8th ed.). Hagerstown, MD: Lippincott Williams & Wilkins.

[12] If you are beginning to exercise for the first time, have not exercised in a while, have a chronic medical condition, or have concerns regarding your ability to exercise, you should contact a primary care physician before embarking on an exercise program. The guidelines offered in this chapter are for the average healthy adult. They do not apply to individuals whose health is compromised. If you have health limitations, your doctor can help develop a plan to fit your situation.

Six: Find Peace and Relaxation

[1] Sapolsky, R. M. (2003). The Physiology and Pathophysiology of Unhappiness. In D. Kahneman, E. Diener, & N. Schwarz (Eds.), *Well-Being: The Foundations of Hedonic Psychology* (pp. 453–69). New York: Russell Sage Foundation.

[2] Sapolsky, R. M. (2003). The Physiology and Pathophysiology of Unhappiness. In D. Kahneman, E. Diener, & N. Schwarz (Eds.), *Well-Being: The Foundations of Hedonic Psychology* (pp. 453–69). New York: Russell Sage Foundation.

[3] Lazarus, R. S. (1999). *Stress and Emotion: A New Synthesis.* New York: Springer Publishing Company.

[4] Cannon, W. B. (1932). *The Wisdom of the Body.* New York: W. W. Norton & Company, Inc.

[5] Biondi, M. (2001). Effects of Stress on Immune Function: An Overview. In R. Ader, D. Felten, & N. Cohen (Eds.), *Psychoneuroimmunology* (pp. 189–226). San Diego, CA: Academic Press.

[6] Pepine, C. J., Abrams, J., Marks, R. G., Morris, J. J., Scheidt, S. S., & Handberg, E. (1994). Characteristics of a Contemporary Population with Angina Pectoris. TIDES Investigators. *American Journal of Cardiology, 74* (3), 226–31.

[7] Becker, L. C., Pepine, C. J., Bonsall, R., Cohen, J. D., Goldberg, A. D., Coghlan, C., et al. (1996). Left Ventricular, Peripheral Vascular, and Neurohumoral Responses to Mental Stress in Normal Middle-Aged Men and Women. *Circulation, 94,* 2768–77.

[8] Blumenthal, J. A., Babyak, M., Wei, J., O'Connor, C., Waugh, R., Eisenstein, E., et al. (2002). Usefulness of Psychosocial Treatment of Mental Stress-Induced Myocardial Ischemia in Men. *The American Journal of Cardiology, 89* (2), 164–68.

[9] Benson, H. (1975). *The Relaxation Response.* New York: William Morrow.

[10] Benson, H. (1984). *Beyond the Relaxation Response.* New York: Times Books.

[11] Benson, H., & Stuart, E. M. (1992). *The Wellness Book: The Comprehensive Guide to Maintaining Health and Treating Stress-Related Illness.* New York: Simon & Schuster.

Seven: Connect with the Creator and Creation

[1] Koenig, H. G. (1999). *The Healing Power of Faith: Science Explores Medicine's Last Great Frontier.* New York: Simon & Schuster.

[2] Mueller, P. S., Plevak, D. J., & Rummans, T. A. (2001). Religious Involvement, Spirituality, and Medicine: Implications for Clinical Practice. *Mayo Clinical Proceedings, 76,* 1225–35.

[3] Myers, D. G. (2000). The Funds, Friends, and Faith of Happy People. *American Psychologist, 55* (1), 56–67.

[4] Luke 6:12–13.

[5] Matthew 14:15–23.

[6] 1 Thessalonians 5:17.

[7] Genesis 2:18.

[8] Genesis 3.

[9] Matthew 22:37–40.

[10] 1 Corinthians 12 and 13.

[11] John 13:34–35.

[12] Romans 5:8.

[13] Romans 8:31.

[14] Matthew 6:25–34.

[15] Philippians 4:4–7.

Staying on Track

[1] Seligman, M. E. (1975). *Helplessness: On Depression, Development, and Death.* San Francisco, CA: W. H. Freeman.